ELLED ACROSS

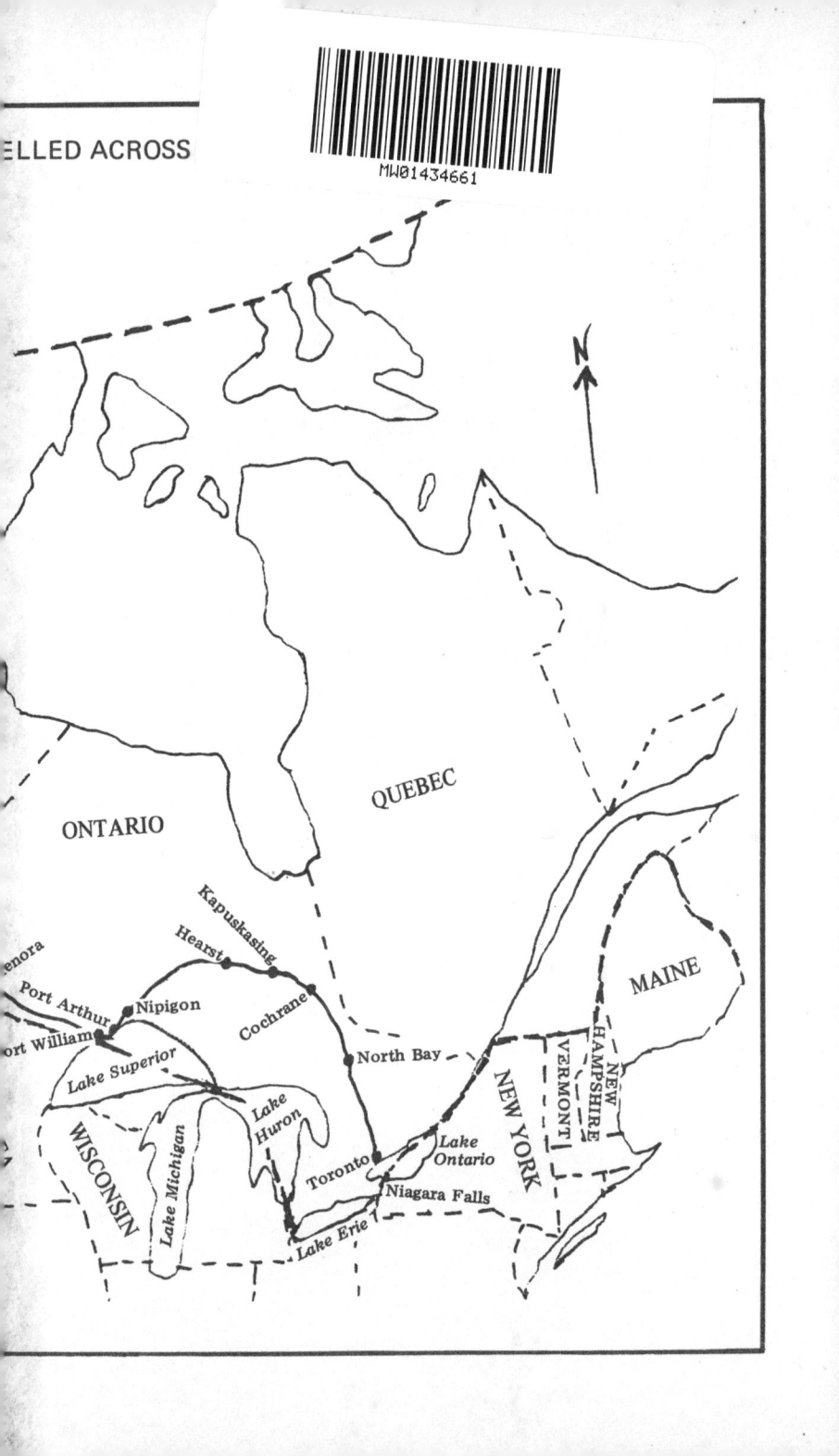

# WHERE THERE'S A WILL

# WHERE THERE'S A WILL
## A Year in Canada
## Mavis Gore

**UNITED WRITERS**
Cornwall

**UNITED WRITERS PUBLICATIONS LTD**
Ailsa, Castle Gate, Penzance, Cornwall.

*All Rights Reserved. No part of this publication may be reproduced, stored in a retrieval system, or transmitted, in any form or by any means, electronic, mechanical, photocopying, recording or otherwise, without the prior permission of the Copyright owner.*

British Library Cataloguing in Publication Data

A catalogue record for this book is available from the British Library.

ISBN 1 85200 057 0

Copyright (c) 1994 Mavis Gore

Printed in Great Britain by
United Writers Publications Ltd
Cornwall

To the memory of my mother and father
and
for Jeff with love

**Chapter One**

August 1st found us at the Canadian Emigration Office. We didn't intend to commit ourselves in any way: it was solely a fact-finding mission. Australia and New Zealand also were seeking people from the British Isles – competition was keen.

Some hours later we emerged, stunned, from Canada House into the afternoon sunshine of London's Trafalgar Square to stand on the pavement surveying each other in disbelief. What had we done? Not only had we agreed to *go* to Canada, but we had signed all the documents necessary for emigrating and we were to travel by the first available ship. *And* we would have to be joined in matrimony before departure: there was a preference for married couples rather than single persons.

Sales talk! Our doubts about the wisdom of emigrating at the beginning of winter, instead of in spring, were swept aside. There was no unemployment. Where had we got that idea? Canada desperately needed to augment her workforce. The country was 'crying out' for folk like us. Thus, we were lulled by a harmonious, drawling voice. Our future was decided!

Jeff and I had been in London since the previous year. Many of our new friends were from overseas and they were willing to endure the privations of life in draughty rooming-houses in their pursuit of 'culture'. Dublin, our home city, one of the oldest in Europe, had plenty of culture of its own. We weren't pursuing . . . just avoiding the displeasure of two sets of parents, who were far from overjoyed at our engagement, but at age twenty-three, we had made our own decisions.

New Zealand was the place which, in the past, had attracted Jeff. He had been considering following a friend there, when he had met me. His plans at first postponed were later abandoned. Now, a couple of years afterwards, I didn't want to go there, and we were not interested in South Africa or Australia, despite the £10 passages on offer. What about Canada? Maybe we would get married early the following year? Jeff would go alone and when he had employment and somewhere to live I would join him. So much for forward planning; our visit to Canada House determined otherwise . . .

Hectic weeks followed our interview. In mid-November we were to sail from Liverpool and before *that* we were to be married. Nothing was easy or straightforward. I wanted a white wedding in Dublin. Arrangements had to be sorted out, parents placated, passports ordered (we applied for Irish ones, though we each had an English parent), trunks acquired, items purchased; all were accompanied by the usual problems, aggravated, in our case, by distance.

Well-meaning friends suggested the type of garments needed. In Canada, these proved to be wrong; however, unaware of this I spent precious time shopping for bargains. It was going to be very cold. On that point everyone was agreed. (I was beginning to wish we were going to Australia after all.) I worked in the office of champagne and brandy importers in Pall Mall – a bit of a waste, because I don't drink alcohol! A colleague, who claimed to have visited Canada many years before, was most vociferous. She suggested that I should buy, no, 'invest in' were her precise words, 'woollen combinations'. Woollen combinations in a bride's trousseau! I almost called off the trip. Even the wedding. I *did* buy woollen vests, heavy sweaters and skirts. Nobody, just nobody, hinted at the fact that anywhere in Canada enclosed by walls and a roof is heated to tropical temperatures.

We had enjoyed life in London making the customary visitor's round of museums, galleries, cathedrals, and in good weather, Kew Gardens, Greenwich, Hampton Court on the periphery. Unlike our overseas friends from their modern cities, we were not agog at the splendour, but we found life interesting. It was possible to travel about relatively easily and cheaply. Public transport was busy, but nothing like today's overcrowded nightmare. Speakers' Corner with its soap-box orators gave us many a Sunday afternoon's free entertainment. In pre-terrorism times, anyone could wander up Downing Street to watch the comings and goings at Number 10. The boss, a proud Londoner, encouraged a colleague from Johannesburg and myself to desert our desks to see special events. In this way we saw the return, with ceremonial pomp, of the Queen and Prince Philip from a successful visit abroad. Another time we viewed the Trooping of the Colour, held then on a weekday. It is an indication of the absence of the now-familiar cordon of police that, by walking briskly along the edge of the pavement, my friend and I were able to keep pace with the Queen when she rode side-saddle on her return along The Mall to the palace. We spent an afternoon at the Chelsea Flower Show, the tickets given to us by the boss. A sop to his conscience? Maybe. He knew that we had noted, when we did the accounts, that his bill for lunch – not dinner! – for two at an exclusive restaurant or club was *more* than either of us got for a week's salary.

In Dublin, going to shows regularly, I was acquainted with many of the theatre personnel from Lord and Lady Longford at the Gate Theatre to the programme sellers in the gods and, though I missed the intimacy of the Dublin theatres and audiences, in London I was in my element. Above all I relished the ballet at Covent Garden and the mesmerising beauty of Margot Fonteyn.

Jeff enjoyed his work as an auto-mechanic. He was absolutely crazy about cars, to the extent that he had given up, after two years, a degree course at Trinity College and, instead, served an apprenticeship in a garage. There was little by way of educational grants in those days; understandably, his parents felt aggrieved at this waste of a university education; but it had happened before his meeting me, so I wasn't blamed for that! In Dublin I was employed in the Civil Service. On deciding to go to London, I thought it would assist my chances of getting a job if I learned how to type. Using an instruction manual, I taught myself on an ancient portable machine, which had once belonged to Margaret Pearse, a sister of the executed 1916 Easter Rising Patriot, Patrick Pearse.

Living together outside marriage was not done. Certainly none of our overseas friends would have considered it, even though they were thousands of miles distant from the watchful eyes of parents. In London, Jeff and I earned average wages yet we found saving a real struggle, therefore the good-humoured hospitality we enjoyed at the home of married friends of Jeff's family, whom we visited two or three times a week, was greatly appreciated. With them we had our first taste of television. ITV was new and popular. Small black and white screens flickering in living-room corners held families spellbound.

None of us living in rooms could afford a set. We couldn't afford much heating either. A gas or electric fire was the only source of warmth, provided the hungry maw of the meter was fed with coins. Often in the evening we would gather in one person's room and share the cost of the fire. I recall a get-together in my friend Blanche's bedsitter. She and Roy were soon to be married. Having come from opposite hemispheres they met while on holiday in Norway, were to be wed in London before going to Canada and eventually, they hoped, to the States. They were due in Toronto a couple of days after our proposed arrival date. Blanche's ugly, pokey room was situated at the top of a tall house. Oxygen masks were distributed on the third landing to assist the final assault on the narrow stairs! Blanche, who was normally of cheerful disposition, was, to put it mildly, very agitated. *Everything* had gone wrong. Her mother was coming from New York the following day and not least of Blanche's worries was: "What will she think of this room?" What indeed! She was, you could say, about to be caught out.

During the evening, as was usual, lively conversation ensued with folk talking about their mundane jobs, their poor accommodation both in London and Europe, when they toured or worked there; their lack of money . . . All the stories, mostly amusing, had the familiar ending, "Gee if the folks back home could see me now," because correspondence only dealt with the bright side of life. Later, in Canada, this experience was repeated; we often heard similar remarks when ex British and Irish bent the truth somewhat, while describing their new life-styles, skirting the unpleasant aspects, in letters to their families.

The first-ever visit of the Bolshoi Ballet to the West was scheduled for London in October. The demand for tickets was enormous despite the exorbitant prices. The hundreds of regulars, who supported Covent Garden — ballet and opera — on a weekly basis, had to take a gamble on getting tickets in competition with those who didn't know the difference between a choreographer and a chiropodist, but wanted to attend because it was newsworthy. We did not get seats! (It was to be another thirty-five years before I saw the Bolshoi: on their home ground in Moscow. Then, ordinary Russians could not afford the tickets, which mostly went to tourists. Our seats were in a box at the side of the theatre; a man made his silent protest at our presence by deliberately blocking our view of the stage, having first trampled on my feet without any apology.)

That autumn, apart from the eagerly awaited Russians, there were other foreign personalities in the news: Egypt's Colonel Nasser, for instance, and the developing Suez Crisis. While I listened to an English office colleague berate Pandit Nehru, the Israelis, Irish Nationalists and Colonel Nasser, all in the same breath, I was conscious of the fact that I was experiencing history in the making; and just as the former three had each contributed nails to the coffin of British Imperialism, in its way, Suez, too, and its outcome, would alter Britain's role as a leading world power, for ever.

My last week in London passed swiftly. Vintage champagne in cut glass goblets for a toast to my future, in the oak panelled main-office, lent a grandeur to the occasion, while I sipped my orange squash!

Afterwards, my friend and I left together. She was shortly to return to Johannesburg. We wondered if our paths would ever cross again.

"See you some day," she called, walking towards Regent Street. I turned down the steps to the underground.

We both loved London; was there a better place to say

au revoir than at Piccadilly Circus?

Our married friends, who had been kindness itself to us during our year-long sojourn in London, were unable to travel to Dublin for our wedding. Their home, where we stowed all our crated stuff for Canada, had taken on the appearance of a warehouse. We bade them a tearful farewell and boarded a train at Euston Station bound for Holyhead. While it chugged northwards through the night my mind, a kaleidoscope of ever-changing pictures of the events of the previous twelve months, helped to pass the journey. Farewell youth! The journey through life was about to begin.

## Chapter Two

Our wedding took place on a day left over from summer — gloriously golden and calm; the gale, which the night before had blown the garage door off its hinges, had died down. My father, looking gravely dignified in his morning suit, was silent during the drive to University Church on St. Stephen's Green, that lovely church built by Cardinal Newman. I knew my father no longer disapproved of my marriage yet his seriousness was awesome. It was not until I myself experienced parenthood, that I understood fully the pain involved in letting go of one's offspring to marriage or emigration.

Following the service, the reception was held in the famous Constitution Room — where the constitution for the new Ireland had been signed — in the Shelbourne Hotel on the other side of The Green.

After a few days, Jeff returned to London for almost a month, while I remained in Dublin. Each passing day brought us nearer to being together again, but I dreaded the agony of parting from my family. Mid-November, the time to leave arrived. It was only the second time in my life I had seen my mother cry — she was usually an exponent of the very English habit of the stiff upper lip. There had been occasions in the past, when someone with less self-restraint would have given way to emotion, but as far as she was concerned, tears were shed in private. Now, she wept bitterly, while holding me in a strangling hug. I felt cruel. In those pre-jumbo jet, pre-package holiday times, people didn't continent hop with the ease, speed and readiness of today, so that, when one said good-bye to one's family and took off for distant lands, it was very solemn, nothing like nowadays' cheerful, cherio-see-you-soon departures.

The harrowing farewells over, a sleepless night on the ferry, then Liverpool, and Jeff to greet me; he had travelled overnight from London. Reliable Jeff, how deeply I loved him. We spent a day in Cheshire visiting my grandparents, also a sister of mine, who was a student nurse. Panic! it was then I realised I had left my trunk keys in Dublin. I had to arrange for them to be sent to Montreal.

The Mersey was bustling with ships, how different from the sad slick of water it is now, when my sister saw us off at the Pier Head on the famous waterfront, under the watchful eyes of the Liver Birds. A brief, tight hug, no words, and she was gone quickly. A sob rose in my aching throat; I choked it down and blinking away unshed tears we went into the embarkation hall.

What seemed like an eternity of discomfort followed. The draughty, barrack-like building was teeming with people, old and young, some happy, others grim-faced. Scores of children were scampering about shrieking, climbing on luggage, falling off, crying, picking themselves up, getting scolded by overwrought parents, dashing about again, stumbling, colliding with each other, bawling open-mouthed, a whirlwind of noise and activity exhausting for children and parents alike. Heaps of baggage of every conceivable size and shape, from smart leather handcases to crates and even barrels boldly marked in big letters, took up much of the floor space. Supposedly, all luggage, other than personal items needed for the voyage, was already stowed in the hold of the ship. Who carried their belongings in barrels I wondered? Obviously people in more straitened circumstances than we were!

At last we boarded *The Empress of Britain*: the name now has the ring of a bygone era. The ship, owned by Canadian Pacific, was the first to be built in Britain with complete air-conditioning, at a cost of six million pounds – a fabulous amount of money. It was but a few months since she had been launched by the Queen.

We were listed for second sitting at meals. Families with children had first sitting: all the waiters dreaded it. We enjoyed our first evening on board. Our second and third, like the days, were spent prostrate on our bunks longing for death having succumbed to the torment of sea-sickness, because we had run into a gale and, despite her twenty-six thousand tons, the ship was thrown about like a child's boat in a bath — anyway, it felt like that to the passengers. During the time we remained in our cabin, our only visitors were the steward and stewardess. The steward merely put in a couple of appearances. He was a small man and, no doubt, felt we were big enough to fend for ourselves; the stewardess, on the other hand, popped in quite frequently.

"Feeling better?" she would enquire in a who's-for-tennis voice.

Grunts from two bunks.

"Good," her hearty reply. Then the door would close and we would be left alone, in semi-darkness.

In our misery, we lost track of time. A shaft of light from the passageway indicated that our cabin door had been opened, but there was no sound for a moment or two, then a gruff man's voice said, "Passports please."

Accustomed to the one and only phrase, "Feeling better?" we weren't prepared for this dramatic change of topic.

"What?" Jeff gasped incredulously, and I knew, in my bottom bunk, from the clarity of the 'what' that he must have raised his face out of the pillow, where he had had it buried for days.

"Passports please."

After a long pause, "What day is it?" Jeff enquired, perplexed.

I think he thought we were already in Montreal!

"It's Sunday evening, Sir," came the patient reply. A lengthy silence ensued. "We left Liverpool on Friday, Sir," said the official in a friendly manner, by way of conversation, I suppose.

After three days I needed to escape the claustrophobic cabin, though my legs still felt wobbly like a newborn foal's. I went to the dining-room for breakfast. There were more empty seats than occupied ones.

"Welcome back!" the waiter teased. Apparently, numbers had dwindled until the previous morning only two persons out of a possible four hundred had turned up for second sitting. Only two! I was mollified to learn that we had not suffered alone during the past couple of days. Even some of the crew had fallen victims to sea-sickness and the nursing staff also had to contend with numerous people who had sustained injuries in falls.

After breakfast I decided some fresh air might revive me a little. I went below. Pulling on an extra sweater, then reaching into the wardrobe for my coat, I said with forced cheerfulness, "I'm going for a blow through on deck. Are you coming?"

"Blow through," Jeff snorted, as if it were a new form of Russian roulette. "Are you mad? I can't even sit up yet," he moaned balefully. "Blow through," he mimicked, "you sound as lively as the stewardess."

He remained in his safe, horizontal position. I took the lift to the boat deck and ventured out.

It was bitterly cold and impossible to stand upright against the force of the icy wind. Some children were endeavouring to play a game with a shuttlecock, but the gale kept catching it and carrying it beyond the reach of their bats. Undaunted, they chased after it, laughing. Great to be young! I turned up the collar of my coat, pulled my scarf tighter and bent almost double, made some stumbling circuits of the ship, before staggering to the companionway and down to the deck below, which was covered in overhead, but open to the sea. I found a vacant seat. The tourist section of *The Empress of Britain* held nine hundred passengers, but not many of them were about on this deck. A steward was pushing the bouillon trolley along. After a bowl of hot soup I sat swaddled in blankets, staring out. The grey sky merged with the grey ocean blurring the distant horizon. Giant waves crashed. One minute I'd be looking up at the leaden sky, the next the ship would have pitched and I'd be gazing down into the turbulent waters of the North Atlantic. Up and down. Up and down. Up and down in a perpetual, creaking, swaying motion, great walls of spray shooting into the air with every lurch of the ship; and my stomach doing somersaults. (Eating that soup was not such a good idea!)

By the afternoon Jeff, too, was upright. That evening, on the way into dinner, we read on the notice-board outside the dining-room that the force 10 storm had lessened and 'a force 9 gale was now blowing with a high sea and a very heavy W.N.W. swell'. Almost all the tables were full. "Welcome back," the waiters teased again. Food had been of little concern during the storm.

Rough seas continued for the remainder of the voyage, but we had got used to the rocking rhythm of the ship. We had found our sea legs. The days were pleasantly punctuated by mealtimes: the food was excellent with plenty of choice; Jeff, and others, quickly made up for lost time. We had an attentive waiter and friendly table companions. The menu cards were interesting. The ones for dinner bore portraits of the first pioneers to explore Canada, accompanied by a resumé of their lives. The lunch-time cards represented modern Canada and each had a coloured photograph of a famous building or place: Quebec's Chateau Frontenac, Toronto's Royal York Hotel, Chateau Lake Louise overlooking Victoria Glacier, Golfing at Banff. The latter two places, we learned, were in the province of Alberta, thousands of miles to the west.

Canada is the second largest country in the world; we were already in possession of that fact, but the stupendous vastness of the country was only beginning to dawn on us. When we stepped on to Canadian soil at Montreal, we would be two thousand five hundred miles from Banff, or the distance from London to Moscow and back. In Montreal we would be further from Vancouver on Canada's other coast, than from Liverpool! From the most easterly to westerly point measures almost five thousand miles. We were realising the gigantic proportions of the landmass we were sailing towards.

"Fat chance we'll ever see 'Golfing at Banff' except on a postcard," I said.

Fate would decide otherwise.

The scheduled six-day crossing grew to seven because of the storm. I didn't make any visits to the hairdresser or beauty salon, but I did buy some cosmetics in the shop. In particular, I remember Elizabeth Arden face powder, in a pretty pink box which resembled a miniature attaché-case. We enjoyed the entertainment on board and became acquainted with some of our fellow passengers. One conversation sowed seeds of niggling anxiety. Our informant was a broadly built Englishman, whose occupation some years before had taken him to Canada, then to Australia and New Zealand. He was bound for Canada again for a brief stay. His reaction on hearing that we were emigrating was to declare brusquely, "You're barmy!"

He considered Canada was finished as a get-rich-quickly-country and as a race Canadians were "only tolerable".

"Why on earth are you coming out at this time of the year?" he questioned. "You should have waited until spring. There won't be any jobs *now*."

That emphatic remark echoed exactly our comments made a few months previously to the Canadian immigration officials in London.

"It all boils down to the climate," he went on. Empty pockets and a hungry stomach are bearable, when you can stretch out on a golden beach and soak up the free warmth, while contemplating how to get a job and accommodation, say, in Australia or New Zealand, but in Canada it's such a different story. There, when the wind whips through the heaviest clothing, you are aware of your empty stomach. I guess that's why Canadians are such an unfriendly shower. The piercing cold makes life outdoors intolerable; nobody lingers to find out how the poor devil just-arrived from Europe is coping. You are so frightfully *alone* when starting life in Canada."

We weren't bent on 'getting rich quickly' but, knowing nobody on the entire North American Continent, we would be alone, and we would need jobs almost immediately. This forecast of life in Canada, coupled with our growing awareness of the vastness of its icy regions was somewhat discouraging, to say the least.

At Father Point, late on Wednesday evening, the pilot joined the ship. Mail and newspapers were taken aboard. My name was called, to report to the purser. I collected a welcome letter from home with my trunk keys. The following morning the ship docked at Wolfe's Cove, Quebec and we adjusted our watches to Eastern Standard Time. We would like to have seen the famous city, regarded by many to be one of the loveliest in the country, but only those disembarking were allowed ashore. Not far away is the battlefield, where, it could be said, the whole future of Canada had been determined when the English finally beat the French and Canada became a British possession.

Immigration officials joined the ship at Quebec and remained with us until we reached our destination, a day later, in Montreal. During that time, in alphabetical order, the passengers were interviewed and our documents and passports examined yet again. All immigrants were given a map of the country with: 'Canada, Things You Should Know', printed in six languages on the cover with basic information written on the reverse of the map.

*The Empress of Britain* would be one of the last ships into Montreal before the port became ice-bound for the duration of the long winter. Quebec would then take over the role of gateway to Canada, until the late spring thaw would unlock the St. Lawrence Seaway again.

At lunch-time on Friday we docked at Montreal. Queuing to disembark proved to be an ordeal equal to that of seasickness. Families with children were first to leave. Had we anticipated the length of time it would take we would have had the presence of mind to borrow a child or two, as it was there was almost time to produce one of our own.

Baggage-encumbered bodies crammed the alleyways. Unable to see the floor in the crush, feet fumbled for each step up the companionways, cases growing heavier while we climbed until, with relief, we could drop them again in a passageway to shuffle along, toeing them in front of us to the next companionway, the next tunnel-like passage, and all the time we were being jostled by crew who darted like moths in and out of cabins checking that nothing had been left behind; others already were stripping the bunks leaving piles of bedding like collapsed tents in each doorway.

Finally, two hours later, we staggered down the gangplank. We were in Canada! What an anti-climax. There was no jubilation at having arrived, only thanksgiving that we had broken through to the real world, shedding the ship like a butterfly escaping its confining chrysalis. We were free!

"Mavis, look! The porters are smoking cigars!" True, many of the dockside personnel were puffing away, the aroma wafting about while they worked energetically, shouting to each other in French, oblivious to the stares of amazement and astonished comments of the newcomers. Neither of us smoke, but if dockers could afford to do so on duty we must be in the land of plenty regardless of our shipboard Job's comforter's opinion, I thought. My spirits lifted, sending a belated excitement coursing through me.

Montreal, though not the capital (Ottawa is) was the biggest city in Canada (now, it is Toronto) and the second-largest French speaking city in the world, but just then all we saw was another gargantuan custom shed, where baggage was grouped alphabetically. We made our way quickly to G division. One by one we located our pieces of luggage and dragged them together, but on reckoning up, a trunk was missing. No cute airport carousels, but mountains of baggage stretched in all directions from A to Z — all the boxes, cases, bags, trunks, barrels, crates and equipment, much of which had already been in the hold of the ship *before* we had entered the embarkation hall in England, plus all the hand luggage.

Like ants we scurried about searching dementedly, stumbling over obstacles, banging our shins, cursing, as we read label after label on trunks which looked similar to our missing one, each time drawing a blank. We split up. I raced down one side. Jeff scoured the other. Dishevelled, we arrived back at G bay, more than half empty now, but still no sign of our trunk.

When it was our turn to be given the third degree, we explained our predicament to the custom's officer.

"I can't clear you until *all* your baggage is here," he said gruffly, in a thick accent, moving away to check someone else's heap of worldly goods.

We made our way back to the gangplank, but were barred from going on board ship again. Were things really so bad in Canada that we were considered potential stowaways — trying to leave the country already, having only experienced the docks? Everywhere, bodies pulled or pushed. Porters' trucks threatened to mow us down as they manoeuvred speedily backwards and forwards between ranges of luggage. We chased after a uniformed figure. Then another. Then another, but always he sped away before we could catch his attention. Eventually, we succeeded. The hold of the ship was searched. No trunk. Jeff and I then started bellowing at each other, which was non-productive, but it helped to relieve our pent-up emotions. The building was clearing fast, the custom's man even more bad-tempered than before.

"You would think it was *our* fault it was missing," I ranted.

The offender was at last found lurking in W bay — it certainly wasn't W for welcome. From there it was trundled by a porter back to G division.

A voice crackled over the Tannoy in English, "Will all passengers for the train to Toronto please assemble outside. The coaches have arrived to take you to the station."

"Heavens, that's us," we gasped.

Transfixing us with a glare, "Not so fast," drawled the official. "You can't leave till I've examined *everything*. No hustle." With what appeared to be deliberate slowness he proceeded to check each item.

Visions of our being stranded in French-speaking Montreal, prompted Jeff to cajole — which he is not usually wont to do! — "Please, can you hurry?"

"What's that?" barked our interrogator eyeing my boxed sewing-machine suspiciously.

"A sewing machine, packed in rubber casing," Jeff tried to remain calm.

"How can I tell it's a sewing machine?"

"We're going to miss that train," I groaned.

Then the ominous words, "Open it."

"We . . . I . . . mightn't be able . . . able to repack it in . . . in time." Jeff was in danger of losing the struggle to control his temper.

"Coaches will leave in five minutes," crackled the voice.

"Okay," grunted the official, suddenly. He marked our luggage and with a flourish signed our papers.

"Porter! Porter, please!"

We raced after them. Seconds later we departed for the station.

We were in no mood to enjoy the sights of Montreal whizzing by. Tired and bedraggled, we needed to slake our thirst and quell our grumbling stomachs. On arrival at the station, trusting to providence that our baggage would be loaded, we climbed aboard the train; the step was much higher than we were accustomed to, and found seats.

Jeff said, "I'll nip across to the coffee stall for some eats." (Having been warned in advance, we knew that having a meal on the train was a luxury we could not afford.)

He hadn't been gone long, when I became aware of many doors slamming in quick succession — we were about to depart. No sign of him. I jumped to the window. Several figures were scampering across the platform, Jeff among them. He clambered on, clutching a carton of coffee in each hand, his pockets bulging with packets of sandwiches; the whistle blew long and shrilly, causing him to slump heavily into his seat, when the train lurched forward Toronto-bound.

Dusk fell; soon the outside world was enveloped in darkness, so we saw little of the countryside through which we travelled, but we were pleasantly surprised at how cleanly spacious the train was; however, our first taste of Canadian heating we found soporific. We dozed intermittently between stops for much of the journey.

About half an hour after midnight, one by one the snoozing passengers came to life and before long confusion reigned as cases were hauled down from racks, bags packed; bodies struggled into overcoats, boots, hats and all the other garments needed to keep the Canadian night-time cold at bay. Jeff drew from his wallet the card bearing our names, which we were to present to an immigration official on arrival at the station in Toronto.

"It's a comfort to know there will be someone to meet us," I said.

"Yes," he replied, repocketing the card, "he will get us fixed up with temporary accommodation."

At the other end of the compartment a child, startled from sleep, began to wail.

"Shush, shush," pleaded the mother, but her voice was drowned in the rising crescendo of sobs.

Four or five toddlers, bulky bundles, waddled up and down the aisle, eyes wide with curiosity. The decibels gradually decreased. Muffled to our ears, our cases by our feet, we sat sheepishly eyeing one another; only a few broke the hush. Children wriggled impatiently to be free, but restraining hands held them in their seats. Mass departures from trains are always the same, I thought — a scramble to be ready on time, followed by an anti-climax of some minutes waiting in awkward silence.

## Chapter Three

The train gradually slowed, then slithered to a stop. Union Station, Toronto. It was Saturday, 24th November, 1956. The time was almost 1 am.

Doors burst open; a mass of bodies and luggage tumbled out at regular intervals down the length of the long train, to be met, at the exit end, by a crowd of people penned in by a railing, their eyes searching, then, on recognising friends, anxious expressions gave way to ones of delight and they waved expansively.

When the barrier was removed they surged forward on to the platform adding to the crush. Kisses. Embraces. Tears were dashed quickly from faces, which incongruously also wore smiles; children were surveyed at arm's length before being scooped into smothering hugs.

"Welcome to Canada!"
"Great to see you."
"Had a good journey?"
"How's the ol' country?"
"Come on, let's go!"

Cases were picked up, bags slung over shoulders; the crowd jostled towards the exits; the clamour abating as it dispersed. For a couple of moments we stood motionless looking on, feeling more than a little helpless and lost. We knew no one in the vastness of Canada's ten million square miles. Near to tears, I felt quite overwrought.

"Better track down the immigration official," Jeff said, a catch in his voice betraying his uncertainty. So, cases in hand, we followed the remnants of the retreating crowd.

A dais marked Immigration Authorities stood forlorn. The

Traveller's Aid was shuttered, also all the kiosks. Ours was the last train.

"Now what?" Jeff muttered, his eyebrows almost meeting in a black frown.

Passengers stood in clusters, about twenty altogether. Abandoned. Perplexed. Several clutched the immigration introduction cards in their hands. A gum chewing official swaggered out of the semi-darkness greeting us like long-lost friends.

"Howde folks?" he purred.

A squeak of a voice — mine! — asked him tremulously if there was an immigration officer on duty.

" 'Fraid not," he replied shaking his head, while chewing. "Left at midnight," chew, chew, "waited as long as he could;" chew, chew, "won't be back 'til Monday mornin'." Violent chewing.

"Monday!" echoed voices in alarm — all the stragglers had gathered round the uniformed dispenser-of-information.

"Well," drawled the Canadian, poking a podgy thumb over a shoulder in the direction of the moribund train, while chewing a bit more, "this here train was late, real late." He stowed his gum in his cheek as he warmed to his subject. "Was doo yesterday. You guys offa *The Empress of Britain?*"

"Yes," we replied like chastened children.

"Shoulda been here yesterday," he lectured.

We did not need to be reminded of *that* fact, nor the storm which caused our delay.

Someone asked innocently, "Any hope of accommodation?"

We were startled when he guffawed with laughter, his large form shaking. I mentally sighed with relief that he had stopped chewing, otherwise he might have choked on his wad of gum.

"It's Grey Cup Day," he declared by way of explaining his mirth.

Blank expressions greeted this utterance. He surveyed us, surprised, then started to chew again.

"Grey Cup Day," he repeated loudly, emphasising each word, between chews.

Glumly, faces gazed at him. The poor chap was visibly

crestfallen on realising that we had never heard of it and, as if to relieve his discomfiture, he chewed vigorously before continuing resignedly, "It's the All Canada Ball Final and this year it's being played in Toronto," — only he pronounced it Tronna — and regaining some of his former self-confidence, he pulled himself up proudly to his considerable height, sticking his chest out as he said, 'Tronna' he went on, "It would be impossible to find anywhere tonight, im-poss-ib-le. City's packed . . . all beds taken."

Travel-pale faces registered understanding. His demeanour changed. Maybe he guessed the All Canada Ball Final was unlikely to be of concern to us early in the morning, nearly fourteen hours since we had docked in Montreal!

He said kindly, "You guys can sleep in the waitin' area if you wanna," and without any more ado he set off briskly like the Pied Piper with us trailing behind, lugging our impedimenta through the station.

We noticed that the place was not bad, not bad at all, but surprisingly modern, spacious, clean and well-docorated throughout. It bore little resemblance to any railway station we had known. Lovely!

"Now ain't that just dandy?" crooned our benefactor, indicating the wooden benches like a commissionaire in a five-star hotel.

There were groans from some when bodies came into contact with unyielding wood; suppressed giggles from others; wails from a couple of children. Occasionally, during what was left of the night, we were disturbed by torchlight — police checking that no undesirables slept in comfort. We newly-arrived immigrants were permitted to stay.

All too soon the waiting-room hummed with activity, with people off the first trains joining those of us who had camped overnight. Young folk bedecked in their teams' colours and brandishing rattles, bounded through the swing doors chanting slogans, oblivious to the prone bodies on the benches. I looked at my watch, 6.10 am. If they could work up such enthusiasm at this hour what would they be like later, I grouched.

We dragged ourselves upright, muscles throbbing in protest. There were washrooms nearby. Never were ablutions more welcome. We tried with little success to shake the creases out of our coats before putting them on and set off in search of food. Our last cooked meal had been twenty-three hours earlier.

When we eventually elbowed our way to the counter of one of the busy coffee stalls, we were bewildered by the array of goodies on offer; items which we might consider for dessert were being offered for breakfast: pancakes with various fillings, a choice of muffins, a riot of doughnuts, sandwiches – double and treble deckers – served on large plates with a knife and fork for attack. With food scarcity still a memory in Europe and limited variety available, we thought we had found the cornucopia. However, even in our ravenous state, pancakes with maple syrup, or any other syrup, or any kind of muffin or doughnut did not appeal to us; instead we settled for something safely commonplace: eggs on toast; but even that necessitated decision, when the girl reeled off the various types of bread on offer and the myriad ways of cooking eggs. Our tea was made with tea-bags. There may have been tea-bags back home, but we had not seen any before our first breakfast in Canada.

In London we had obtained the address of an organisation that offered to help immigrants; their office was in Yonge Street. Duly fortified, we decided to make our way there, having ascertained where Yonge Street was; but first we had to see to our heavy baggage, which was being unloaded from the train. To our dismay, the side of one of our trunks had caved in, the one that held most of our wedding presents – all the wealth we possessed in the world. Squashed cartons could be seen through the rent, but because we were powerless to do anything about it just then, we booked everything into left-luggage and hoped nothing would go missing, while the damaged trunk languished there.

Beyond the glass doors of the station, the street was busy with traffic. Sun blazed in an azure sky. Jeff pushed open the door and I preceded him outside. Brrr what a shock! The cold stunned us after the warmth inside.

"But it looks lovely!" I spluttered in disbelief.

Sunshine is usual in winter in Canada, but sun was not to be equated with heat. It was freezing, literally. We crossed a street, wide compared with European streets, the far pavement quite a distance away. In our anxiety to reach it we forgot, until a blare of raucous horns from cars, which threatened to mow us down, reminded us, that traffic travelled on the right side of the road, and fast. How fast! The tooting of horns was to let us know we were law-breakers. Jaywalking is a finable offence in Toronto. All road crossings must be made at intersections.

On reaching the safety of the pavement (sidewalk in Canadian parlance, they call the road: pavement) we stood watching the passing vehicles; huge, bright-coloured, steel monsters with large fins, whose names had a romantic thrill, Cadillac, Pontiac, Chevrolet, none of the drab reconditioned midgets that we were accustomed to in Ireland and Britain, where, though petrol was no longer rationed, car-ownership was only for the better-off. Wide roads for big cars; Toronto, like the rest of North America, was a car-owning community.

Turning up a side street, we gasped as an eye-stinging wind whipped our breath from us. The sky-scraper buildings create wind tunnels down which the Arctic blasts hurtle headlong towards the Great Lakes. Already our teeth were chattering like castanets. We took refuge in a café, where we were grateful for the stifling air which enveloped us as we passed through the door, but within minutes, before we had time to be served, we felt uncomfortably hot; my wool vest, bought in London at a friend's behest, was sticking to my back; we ventured outdoors again.

"Everyone here, in time, must die from pneumonia," I stated emphatically. "I don't know how they get used to the extremes of heat and cold."

In the café the wall thermometer had read eighty Fahrenheit, while the street temperature registered on huge thermometer-cum-clocks high on several buildings was twenty-four: eight degrees of frost.

"Let's go to this office in Yonge Street," Jeff said impatiently. We found ourselves in Toronto's famous thoroughfare. "No need to take the subway, might as well walk; it can't be far." Little did we know that Yonge Street (with a change of name) is fifty miles long, all the way to Lake Simcoe. Honestly! The longest street in the world? Running due north, it is, without doubt, the coldest and windiest!

"Watch out for bears. We must be nearing polar regions. What number have we reached?" I stammered through teeth making staccato sounds like crockery on a vibrating trolley.

But our long trek had been in vain. The office was closed. We blasted the five-day working week. Britain had not yet adopted the custom universally with many offices working half-day on Saturday, consequently we had not expected this.

"I'm frozen," I moaned. "Let's go back to our friendly neighbourhood station. Can we get a street-car? We've already walked miles."

It was only then that we became aware that there was no traffic moving. Along the edge of the pavement on both sides of the road spectators were gathering; from all the side streets good-humoured crowds converged on Yonge Street.

"Imagine turning out in such force to welcome us," Jeff quipped, bowing to right and left. Had he turned cartwheels or walked on his hands he would not have attracted the slightest attention from the crowd who, jostling one another for kerbside vantage points, strained their necks looking up the street in excited anticipation. How could we have forgotten? It was Grey Cup Day! The crowd was here to see the pre-match parade. Most were wearing the colours of one or other of the teams: The Montreal Alouettes and The Edmonton Eskimos (now it is considered insulting to use the word Eskimo; the people who live in the frozen wastes are called Inuit); and it was not children alone who carried rattles and streamers. If it had not been for the misery-making cold we would have enjoyed the carnival atmosphere.

For a while we continued to make our way down Yonge Street but we had to concede defeat when the throng grew denser. What a procession it proved to be, taking an hour and a half to pass, a lavish spectacle of colour and beauty. It must have cost a fortune and taken months of planning. I could not understand how the participants, particularly those sitting or standing immobile in the various tableaux, did not freeze to death. Ice maidens!

After the last float with its accompanying troupe of smiling girls had swept smoothly past and all the short-skirted, baton-twirling majorettes had high-stepped out of sight to the strains of the last band, now faint in the distance, the crowds from the pavements spilled on to the wide roadway and like a colourful river flowed after the procession. At least we were being propelled in the direction we wanted to go; in my case I was being carried, clinging heavily to Jeff, my legs dragging along the pavement.

"My legs, there is no feeling in them at all!" I gabbled.

From the knees down I was numb.

In the afternoon a girl in The Travellers' Aid in Union Station booked a room for us in a small hotel. We collected our overnight cases from left-luggage, hailed a cab, and within a few minutes — having travelled up Yonge Street yet again — we were there. On inspection we found the room tiny, but it was all that was available.

"English?" inquired the receptionist, in a thick European accent, when we signed the register. "Our charge is for room only and does not include breakfast." (Not bed and breakfast, just bed, but that would be an improvement on a hard bench.) "We haven't a dining-room here, but there are restaurants in Yonge Street. Do you know Yonge Street?"

"Yes," we answered truthfully, it being the only street we knew in the whole of North America!

What seemed in Britain to be a substantial amount of money (and we had brought more than the minimum suggested by Canadian Emigration) here was worth considerably less. To conserve our funds while passing the time, we wandered around the three department stores: The Hudson Bay, Eatons and Simpsons, not doing any buying, just looking; but, apart from the abundant variety of foodstuffs, there was little to admire. After London's West End it was so mundane, so provincial, so small . . . *This* was Toronto? Light years away from Metro, as the city is now proudly referred to by its inhabitants. Above ground its public buildings and shopping malls are eye-catching, but it is its subterranean community that makes the modern city unique. It has probably the largest pedestrian underground walkway in the world with three miles of tunnels and seven subway stops, yet uniform heating, air-conditioning, lighting, water gardens, and ornamental trees contribute to the illusion that it is in the open air. Not so much a Cinderella transformation for Toronto more a Liza Doolittle one.

But there was no hint of the wonders of the future on that Grey Cup afternoon in our adopted city. Indoors, we found the heat very overpowering and frequently we had to escape to the street to be revived by gulps of icy air; then, when the cold crept through the crevices of our woollen armour, we would go back into the shops again to thaw out; thus the afternoon dragged by.

"That's been the longest day of my life," Jeff groaned that evening.

He was wrong. Very wrong! We had not yet suffered a *Sunday* in Toronto.

Next morning, following Mass at St. Michael's Cathedral — comforting in its familiarity — we wandered the bleak streets, there was none of the previous day's sunshine, looking for somewhere we could assuage our hunger. It was as if the city had died overnight, not a soul on foot. Broken rattles, abandoned sashes: yesterday's decorations were today's debris. Paper streamers fluttered in gutters, a baby's shoe in the middle of a wide pavement.

At last we found a diner open. It was straight out of an old-time American movie: outside, a dark green painted pailing and some wooden steps, inside, more dark green paint on floor and benches. The backs on the latter were so high that they divided the space into booths. The tables were covered with checked cloths reminiscent of cowboy shirts, but this was no Western saloon, oh no! At that time in Toronto, there were only six licenced restaurants in the entire city and this wasn't one of them! The menu was chalked on a huge board. We were so cold and hungry that anything, regardless of content, would have been welcome provided it was hot. It *was* hot, plenty of it and appetising, a traditional roast meal, though it was only late breakfast time.

How were we going to spend the rest of the day? Where could we go? Everywhere, just everywhere, apart from a few eating establishments, was closed. There were no Sunday newspapers. We could not believe it. Sunday newspapers were published on a Saturday, bulky monstrosities, full of advertisements, sport reports and comic strips, but on our first Sunday in Toronto we could not find anywhere open to buy one. *News*papers sold a day in advance!

Memories of Sundays spent enjoying Dublin's or London's attractions did not help. Escaping the drizzle, in sympathy with our mood, we returned to the hotel to peruse some back numbers of Readers' Digest, the only reading matter to hand, apart from the Gideon's Bible; neither was there a television or radio. We emerged once more to have a late lunch/early supper; then bought some milk, packaged sandwiches and fruit to stave off future hunger; considering ourselves lucky to have found a shop open in the Toronto wasteland, we retreated to the warmth of our den.

Afterwards, on hearing the Canadian joke, "I spent a week in Toronto one Sunday," we could answer from experience, "Brother, so did we!" (Another joke which was doing the rounds at that time was: "First prize, a week in Toronto; second prize, two weeks!")

On arrival at the Department of Immigration on Monday, we joined a score shivering in the rain in the street outside the office, which had not opened. When it did, the waiting area filled and the sodden mass drying out contributed to the rising humidity!

Some stood in clusters chatting; others, faces drawn, sat silently.

"Central Europeans, probably Hungarians," Jeff whispered.

It was but a few weeks since the uprising in that unhappy land. Refugees! Overwhelmed with compassion for them, for a while I forgot that we, too, were homeless. Canada was offering them sanctuary as she had done to countless displaced persons in the past. On the world scene, the country was becoming much more politically assertive than previously, which was shown in the prominent role the country was playing during the Suez crisis, and whose constructive ideas were recognised when, later, the Nobel Peace Prize was awarded to the minister of External Affairs, Lester B. Pearson.

I felt certain Canada offered us all a good future. But while these lofty thoughts were floating around in the back of my mind, the front was more occupied with the here and now: for instance, we were still a long way down the queue; the room was stuffy; lunch-time had come and gone without sustenance and we had only had fruit and milk in our room for breakfast — it was time to call it a day.

Out into the teeming rain to return to the offices which had been closed on Saturday. There, we were given details of a furnished flat not far from down-town Toronto and an appointment was made by 'phone for us to view it. The girl assured us that it was 'quite inexpensive'. During the following weeks we discovered that a Canadian's idea of inexpensive and a newly-arrived immigrant's, with funds in European currency, were poles apart. Everything in life is relative. One lives and learns and for the next few months we newcomers learned a great deal, often quite painfully.

We were directed where to get a street-car. Street-cars: a more uncomfortable mode of transport doesn't exist! Dusk had fallen when we alighted, making it difficult to find the house — a small, single-storeyed shop occupied the space where we expected the house to be. Jeff's mood was blackening. Creeping furtively along a passageway beside the shop we came to a flight of steps running up the side of the building to a door.

"Here we are!" I chirped on mounting the steps and reading the number in the half-light.

We rang the bell. But that makes it seem quick and easy, which it was not. The nine steps were narrow and without a handrail; there was just about room for both of us on the top platform, but we could not discern how callers attracted the occupant's attention, because there was no bell or knocker; however, when our eyes grew accustomed to the gloom, we realised that there was a layer of glass (perspex) between us and the front door. Our first storm door! These protective screens, a type of double glazing, were fitted on the outside of doors and windows in winter, to be replaced in summer by ones of wire gauze, permitting windows and doors to be left open, while affording security from intruders, not least flies and mosquitoes.

The discovery was made that storm doors open outwards, when we almost backed into space to avoid it, as it swung towards us to reveal a door with a bell. I pressed it, but our skirmish with the screen had heralded our arrival; the door was opened immediately and, before we uttered a word, a female voice — in the dimness we could not see the speaker — shrilled, "Say, guess you've come about the apartment. Come on in. Sure been a bad day. So you folks have jus' arrived from the Ol' Country. Now isn't that swell? Jus' swell," She pulled the storm-door to and latched it then closed the front door. By the hall light I could see she was middle-aged, thin, nervy-looking.

"Sure hate the cold," she complained rubbing her bare arms, I noticed she was wearing a sleeveless, silk dress at the end of November, while I was attired in layers of wool, the customary protection at home against the *indoor* cold!

"I'll show you the apartment."

We still hadn't breathed a word. What if we were not prospective tenants? We proceeded to wipe our feet on the hall mat.

"Oh, oh, please take off your boots . . . sure make a mess, you know, dirties the rugs. Rather you jus' wore pumps 'round the house, up and down the stairs and all that you know."

Pumps? Did she mean tennis pumps? Before I could ask what the 'all that' referred to, she was speaking again.

"I like to keep the place nice, you know," — we hadn't known, but we certainly did now — "the rugs, the stairs . . . "

I daren't look at Jeff for fear of laughing. On removing our footwear, feeling rather sheepish in our stockinged feet, we followed in her wake, not seeing anything of the much-treasured rugs (we discovered Canadians call carpets rugs) because the hall was covered entirely by sheets of clean newspaper.

"Call me Ella, my husband's name is Jim," she called over her shoulder, darting upstairs.

No surname. Bosom pals already. Maybe the newspapers were a sign of welcome, like a red carpet or something?

"Jim's family came from Liverpool, mine from Scotland. But that was way back."

She made it sound like medieval times. The prospect of having somewhere to stay was such a relief that we didn't notice much, except that the rooms were small — well to be honest, minute. How pleasure could temporarily have blinded us I'll never know. We *did* notice that despite the bathroom's Lilliputian dimensions it had four or five rails each draped with precisely folded hand towel, guest towel and face flannel in lace-trimmed pale lavender and toilet rolls in the same shade. Back home there wasn't much available in the way of lace-trimmed towels for everyday use and with paper products still scarce toilet paper was, for the most part, definitely of the utility kind – shiny, scratchy and strongly smelling of disinfectant.

Early the following morning we arranged for our baggage to be moved to Ella's – we still did not know her surname. We left lively Union Station, which had been our base for our first three days in the New World and would you believe, it was twenty-five years before we entered it again.

Next, we returned to the immigration office, going part of the way by subway, a vast improvement on street-car travel. Today, Toronto is served efficiently by a network of underground trains, but then there was only one short line, opened a couple of years previously, north-south under Yonge Street. It made a pleasant change to be travelling in comfort *under* the street.

Another tedious wait. At last we were ushered into a cubicle. Jeff handed over our papers and introduction card, which were given back after a perfunctory glance.

"Well, what brings you here?" the tall Canadian asked, pushing his chair away from his desk, stretching his legs to relax them.

We explained that we had been instructed in London to report there and began to explain about Saturday and Monday, but we were cut short by the interviewer.

"Ah," he drawled, retracting his long legs and sitting upright. "There's no need for you guys to come here. Take a look, we're busy placing DPs (Displaced Persons). You speak English. Surely you can fend for yourselves?"

This question was uttered sharply implying that we were damned nuisances to be there wasting his valuable time. The realisation that *we* had been wasting *our* valuable time – two whole days – goaded us to ask, "Why were we told we *had* to report here?"

"I dunno," he said, accompanied by a shrug of his

shoulders, "sometimes they (the emigration officers in England) are a bit out of touch with conditions here."

We had reason to recall that comment, because there were many demonstrations that 'they' were unaware of the rapidly changing conditions for immigrants in Canada, owing to the exceptionally large number of Europeans entering the country. The few months preceding and after our arrival, saw the greatest influx of immigrants since the 1930s.

During the afternoon our luggage arrived from the station. The smallness of our two rooms soon manifested itself when we kept falling over each other while unpacking. On emptying our damaged trunk it was a relief to find that there were only a couple of breakages; nothing was missing. With Jim's help the cases and trunks were stored in the attic. Now at least we had somewhere to live though we were both jobless.

Employment was an urgent priority. There was no labour exchange or equivalent and we had drawn a blank at immigration. Talking to Ella and Jim confirmed our suspicions that there was far from an abundance of jobs. If Canada was the place of opportunities there were not many available just then! At times we wondered what country the Canadian Emigration Officers had had in mind, when they interviewed us in London. Somehow the reality didn't bear any resemblance to the promised land they had forecast. Advertisements in newspapers in addition to making the usual demands for qualifications and references, required licences. Whatever *they* were we definitely hadn't got them. Even a lift-attendant would have his certificate proudly displayed declaring so and so 'is authorised to operate this elevator'. It was a vicious circle. You could not get work without a piece of paper to prove you had been trained to do it; and you could not acquire a certificate until first gaining experience in Canada. A licence proved the owner had passed a written test of competence to perform a job; it was also an entitlement to recognised rates of pay.

Jeff set out job hunting — again! With no employment centres or labour exchanges and no advertisements for suitable vacancies in the newspapers, he vowed he would walk the streets of Toronto until he found work. I rattled by street-car across the city to meet Blanche, who had phoned on receiving the letter I had left for her at the American Express office. They were staying at a youth hostel. Roy, too, was out scouting for work. Blanche was inconsolable. Her father, whom she had not seen for three years had met their ship in New York and was greatly distressed that they were unable to delay in the USA because Roy had no visa. Poor Blanche was suffering the pangs of homesickness, which was infectious and I ended up feeling even more sorry for myself than I had been before meeting her.

While we bemoaned our fate, another woman, about thirty-five, came into the communal kitchen. We introduced ourselves. Her name was Eva. She was a Czechoslovakian married to an English man, Benjamin, also out looking for employment; they had two children, Sara aged nine and Jamie, eighteen months. All three of us were newly-arrived from London, by different sea routes, yet none of us was English born.

Eva moved about the cramped room making preparations for lunch, which was no straightforward matter: there was a paucity of kitchen equipment and utensils. Her sentences kept trailing off as she knelt down to peek into low cupboards or clambered on to a rickety stool to peer into top ones; but in the end it had to be stew, because, in spite of her search, she could find only one saucepan. She was petite. Her almost black eyes emphasised the paleness of her face which, with its high cheek bones and generous mouth in a frame of dark hair, was not beautiful, but its composure seemed born out of hardship, maybe sorrow? Her modulated voice bore only a trace of an accent and when she spoke her small hands fluttered gracefully accentuating her words. Regardless of her unfashionable clothes and shabby surroundings, she was quite a lady, though unaware of the impression she created, I'm sure, while cheerily cooking her concoction.

Roy returned. He was stiff with the cold but still jobless. He was followed shortly by Eva's husband, Benjamin. With his coat collar turned up, hat well pulled down, dark horn-rimmed glasses perched on his blue-with-the-cold nose he surveyed us in disgruntled silence, before shaking his head in answer to Eva's question. He, too, was jobless. We commiserated with each other.

On my return to the flat, I was greeted by Jeff in jubilant mood — or as jubilant as his frozen flesh allowed — because shortly he would join the ranks of the employed as a motor mechanic. He had gone from place to place *on foot* in the bitter weather, covering about six miles of pavement, asking for work and arrived at the opportune moment at a garage that was short-handed. They didn't insist on a licence. He was to start work in a few days. Not the best of jobs, but anything was welcome. It was a relief. We had made deep inroads into our small capital.

The following morning, Friday, we sallied forth to shop for groceries. We had bought very little since arriving, but with the prospect of a future wage, we decided to get some food. Supermarkets were not widespread in Britain and those already in existence were usually on a small scale. Not so in Toronto. First, there was the enormous parking lot with its outdoor children's playground — nothing that size back home; then through the automatic plate-glass doors — a touch of the abracadabra, they opened by magic — into the spacious, brilliantly lit interior with its maze of aisles, abundance of goods, piped music plus attractive coffee shop. We were spellbound by the range and choice of goods on offer and the way certain commodities were sold in much larger packs than we were accustomed to: milk in huge cartons with such variety, homogenised, skimmed, low fat, extra creamy, orange, chocolate flavoured . . . we were used to milk, plain in half pint or pint bottles, not cartons, and you could only get it when an empty bottle was exchanged for a full one! (Back home, a refrigerator was regarded as a luxury, rather than an essential item of kitchen equipment, as it was in Canada; therefore perishable foodstuffs were bought only in small quantities as needed.) Sugar was packed in five pound bags; grapefruit, oranges, apples in big, net sacks; of course, tea-bags; absolutely giant containers of washing powder; the first boxes of *coloured* tissue handkerchiefs we had seen. And what was this? Yes, toilet paper like Ella's in all the hues of the rainbow. Unbelievable luxury! Everything was attractively packaged and displayed. We were greatly impressed.

We staggered back to the flat, our purchases in stout brown paper sacks — given free. Though it was some time since rationing in the UK and Ireland many things were still scarce; in particular there was a dearth of paper and wrappers. We stowed everything away; counted our remaining cash — not a great deal left! It was noon. Exactly a week since we had docked at Montreal. It felt more like half a lifetime.

## Chapter Four

'You may find your first Canadian job not exactly what you had planned, but you would be wise to accept the employment offered . . . ' ran the blurb, in six European languages, in the Information Section on the reverse of the map of Canada, that we had been given on board ship.

I don't know about wisdom, more likely necessity proved the spur; but within two weeks we each had a job of sorts, apart from Eva who, because of the children, was not looking for paid work. (After meeting her with Blanche, in the hostel kitchen, friendship between the six of us had developed quickly.) Outdoor seasonal employment had finished, consequently in town there were many chasing each vacancy; the less mentally-demanding the position the greater the number pursuing it. The licence was a prerequisite. No scrap of paper. No job.

Neither the appalling shortage of employment nor these wretched licences had been mentioned to us. In London, when we had suggested that it was inappropriate to arrive in Canada in winter, we had been assured there was nothing to worry about: there was plenty of work. Well there wasn't! But here we were. Now we had to make the best of it. More often it was a case of not getting any job than on securing the one 'you had planned'! We were amazed at the amount of paper work involved in the simplest transaction; and the detailed questionnaire accompanying a job application could be mind-boggling. Non-English or non-French speakers found it most difficult of all. It was as if their earlier life did not matter; as if they had only become persons on arrival in Canada, having previously lived on a different planet. We met a former judge employed as a joiner; others who had been lawyers, medical doctors, architects, teachers . . . in Europe, were glad to do menial jobs in Canada, once they had qualified for their certificate. These European professionals could be forgiven for thinking they had been 'imported' for jobs Canadians didn't want.

Canada was not a homogeneous society: there were too many cultures for that; it was not a melting pot like the USA. It was a land of pioneers: a tough, independent, courageous people — a nation of individuals. They were (and are still) fiercely proud of that. Of course, it is not just a country, but a continent of outrageous dimensions, with six time zones. Spread over enormous distances, its small population — 15 million then, 25 now — mostly live in a string of cities from East to West, the majority of which are within two hundred miles of the US border, thus many are situated considerably closer to an American city than they are to their nearest Canadian one. Such distances make it difficult, not only for the transportation of commodities, but more so for ideas and emotions. Big news in the area in which it happens is hardly mentioned outside it. Today, nearing the end of the century, the diversity of languages is causing an educational barrier necessitating the introduction of literacy programmes right across Canada, because it is estimated that one adult in five (many of them born in the country) has difficulty in reading English. But I digress!

Blanche and Roy moved to a lovely apartment in North Toronto; with the propinquity of the States and Blanche's parents in New York, they were not obsessed with economising for fear of running out of cash; but with Sara and Jamie in tow, Eva and Ben were finding it difficult to get somewhere to live. The hostel became our meeting place, where we got together frequently to compare achievements, or have a moan. It was not customary to accept children in these establishments, but they had been wardens in various British hostels, so the Canadian hostel waived its rule in their favour. Their upstairs room was carpeted; it had divans, easy chairs, the ubiquitous closet (walk-in cupboard) and two kitchen chairs, accommodating us all at a squeeze. The children were usually in bed by the time we got there, but if not, they were always well-behaved.

One of my first memories of Ben was in this room. Arriving tired from work, hungry, he sat straddling one of the wooden chairs, the other drawn up in front of him acting as a table for his dinner plate, which had been borne triumphantly from the downstairs kitchen by Eva who, on acquiring extra saucepans, had graduated from stew to more adventurous fare. Ben, nostrils twitching at the aroma, bent his tall frame over the 'dining' chair, pleasure manifesting itself on his cold-pinched face.

"Ah! Food!"

He made to pick up something with his fork, but it came up empty, while the big, tin plate of dinner began to rotate. Politely, nobody passed any comment. Conversation flowed uninterrupted. The plate slowed to a gentle revolution. Ben stabbed at the food, but again the fork, acting like a starting handle, sent it spinning crazily like a child's top, but it didn't impale anything. Waiting for it to slow down he continued to chat, his lack of concern suggesting that revolving dishes were commonplace. He took aim. His fork grated on tin. The plate spun. Still talking, though no longer waiting for his dinner to come to rest, he prodded again and again with a vigour born of frustration: all to no avail. Resignedly he laid down his knife and fork. We exploded with laughter.

"Eat American style," Roy advised.

Cutting up his food like a child's, Ben then transferred his fork to his right hand, steadying his plate with his left, he proceeded successfully to finish his first course and on to his dessert. Declaring that he felt a new man, he moved across the room to sit on the end of one of the divans, leaned back against the wall, took a small, tin box from his pocket and lit a custom-made cigarette. He sat in contented silence for a minute or two watching the smoke eddying ceilingwards. Then, he laughed uproariously, not looking at any of us, but still gazing at his cigarette smoke. Conversation stopped. We looked at him in surprise.

"What's the joke?"

"Gosh!" he replied, shaking his head in incomprehension. "What awful jobs we immigrants accept."

"Why? What work are you doing?" Roy enquired.

"Cutting washers."

"Washers! What sort of washers?"

"Big, flat, cardboard washers," Ben enunciated each word slowly. "It requires terrific concentration," he continued earnestly.

"Does it?" Blanche blurted, taking him seriously, still, after three years of exposure to it, unattuned to British irony.

"Oh yes, I pull a lever with my right hand, press another with my left foot again and again, a thousand times . . . who knows? . . . maybe a million times a day."

We all giggled, including Blanche.

"Just think," Ben went on, "the sense of achievement I get at the end of the day, when I survey my heaps of cardboard washers. All perfect. Not one differing from another by the merest thousandth of an inch. Such precision. Marvellous! Staggeringly satisfying isn't it? On the street-car tonight I had to put my right hand in my pocket — kept reaching up for the lever . . . instead, knocked the hat of the woman in front."

"But I thought you were working in a garage?" Jeff said, when the merriment subsided.

"I was," Ben replied, "lasted for a day — all day Saturday. Phew! It felt like a week. What slavery!"

At that time none of us had heard of 'a minute car wash'. Ben enlightened our darkness. Split second timing being important, the men were chosen for dexterity and strength. Cars entered the garage in a continuous stream on a conveyor belt, bumper to bumper (fender to fender to use our newfound American English). The team consisted of seven stalwarts, who stood in readiness in three pairs facing each other across this belt with the extra man in front. When a car approached he bounded in, arms swinging in a circular movement. Nifty was his middle name. No fumbling footer he. After cleaning the windows he emerged seconds later rump first. By that time the next car would be in position, with a spring into the vehicle, do the windows, a leap backwards through the door, and so on and on and on . . . With hoses the first pair sloshed down the vehicle with water, while the next two, armed with two giant chamois leathers held one in each hand at arm's length between them, dried it.

Their movements had to synchronise when they drew the two chamois across bonnet (hood) roof (top) boot (trunk) and to the next pair, who cleaned the wheels, doors and outside of the windows; then the car gleaming with goodness rolled off the conveyor belt . . . all in the space of one minute.

Ben was one of the duo who held the chamois. After a while he said their arms ached at being held aloft, but they were kept in that position by the tautness of the cloths. If one had slackened his hold the other's arms would have fallen lifeless to his sides. Forwards and backwards, forwards and backwards, grunt and grunt, grunt and grunt, it wasn't long before he was gasping for a cigarette. Though still a novice, for the sake of economy, he was rolling his own. But how to make a cigarette with hands that were only available for a second at a time? He gave us a spirited demonstration of how he persevered, despite swallowing paper, burning his upper lip and choking on some tobacco. The gang were paid only while there was work. In the idle intervals, Ben practised his cigarette construction. A dozen hung about the garage eager for a job, eyeing each other suspiciously wondering which lucky seven would make up the next team. When sufficient cars were waiting, the boss would stride among the work-hungry men making his selection: "You . . . you . . . you . . . " and the others would fall back dejectedly, but ever hopeful that next time they would be chosen. It says something for Ben's stamina that always he was picked, but one day was enough! He had perfected his technique and was creating cigarettes for the sheer pleasure of achievement, not because he needed a smoke. He considered his day well spent.

We were not long in Toronto before realising how inappropriate our clothing was. It was necessary to be dressed for great extremes of cold and heat. Outdoors that winter it seldom rose above freezing; usually, too, there was a bitter wind that flicked the skin with the precision of a cheese slicer. Canadians wore fur or fur-lined coats (no animal liberation then) or coats lined with a special material impervious to wind; but our overcoats were not suitable armour against the rigours of Arctic cold. To compensate for the inadequacies of mine I used to wear underneath it: sweaters, heavy skirts, and, until I learned better, wool underwear; with scarves, hat, gloves I was ready, if not to brave the elements, at least to sidle out. In Dublin I had bought long fur boots, which I had donned during our first day in Toronto and for four months I wore them whenever I ventured outdoors. Despite the clobber, after only brief exposure, I would shrivel miserably. Poor Jeff suffered badly, too, though he is a more warm blooded creature than I am. He bought a hat with earmuffs, which at least kept his brain alive, and overshoes to wear in rain, later in snow.

We travelled to work by street-car. A network of cars served the city and though they were frequent, journeys were slow, dependent on making several changes. Aboard I would be in a crush, alight at an intersection to change direction, await another vehicle, then, when almost turned to a pillar of ice, scramble up the steps, soon to reach melting point again, until decanted near the office.

On going indoors what an atmospheric transformation! Canadians, who never do anything by halves, keep thermostats set at high; but worse than the heat was the airlessness. Clad as I was, wearing everything except a bearskin, soon I was suffocating. First my gloves, then scarves would be removed; a few gasping minutes later I would unbutton my coat; if circumstances permitted I would shed it; but still I sweltered and would remove a sweater or two until I had divested as far as decency allowed, but there was no combating the lack of air. Picture me — even in church — on the point of expiration, surrounded by an array of discarded garments, but still wearing my detestable boots. A sense of dignity had given way to a sense of survival. I could not determine which I loathed more: the cold outside or the airless heat indoors!

My colleagues in the office wore lightweight dresses. Back home, harkening to the advice of friends, blithely I had given away my summer frocks. I had seldom needed them in the British Isles; who would have thought I would have wished them back in the depths of a Canadian *winter?* Now there was no spare money to buy clothing.

Wanting to be acquainted with our surroundings, at weekends we found our way about Toronto, using the uncomfortable street-cars; they were cheap and our customary way of getting to know places by walking would have taken an eternity: the streets were miles long and distances between places of interest, great. Like most North American cities, Toronto is built on a grid pattern. Situated on the north shore of Lake Ontario, one of the Great Lakes, so huge it resembles a sea, the city rocketed to success following the discovery of fabulous mineral resources in the Province of Ontario — gold, silver, cobalt, uranium . . . These minerals were regarded as the pillar of the Canadian economy.

Wide, attractive University Avenue has, apart from Canada's largest university, several famous hospitals and the brownstone Romanesque buildings set in landscaped grounds of Queen's Park, seat of the provincial parliament. I suppose you could call it Toronto's most important thoroughfare, which is not the same thing at all as saying it is the richest! That is Bay Street with its skyscraper buildings containing the offices of the numerous mines. The twenty-storeyed Royal York Hotel, with its uniformed attendant known as a bell-hop, had twelve hundred rooms, making it, at that time, one of the largest in the Commonwealth, though, in our impecunious state, all we ever saw of it was the outside. Living accommodation for the most part was in apartment blocks or detached houses with open gardens — no walls or hedges — giving an air of spaciousness; some of these homes were magnificent. There were many trees. Yet despite Toronto's wealth, its teeming life in the city centre, almost as hectic as New York's with its overwhelming sense of traffic, it struck us as being simply a boomtown on a large scale. In a letter home I wrote, 'It's lacking in character, and charm; balanced between the British way of life and the American, it doesn't seem to have developed any individuality of its own.' That was not being too harsh, really — Canadians, themselves, called it Hogtown!

Eva and Ben exchanged living at the hostel for the doubtful advantage of renting a cramped flat, where a single bed, two dilapidated armchairs, an eyesore of a gas stove, all of which should have been relegated to the scrap heap years before, but had been kept by an enterprising landlord, now justified the epithet part-furnished being applied to otherwise empty rooms. They bought furniture on credit and, remarkably, managed to create the semblance of a home.

With Blanche and Roy, we got together frequently in their small living-room, to sit talking. It was only a matter of weeks since we had first met, yet we felt as though we had known them for ages. In London, we could have been next-door neighbours of theirs for years and never got past the 'good morning' stage. (A colleague of mine there had mentioned in conversation once that she had lived for seventeen years beside her neighbours and had never spoken to them! How is that for British reserve?) Meeting as we did, when we were jobless new arrivals in Toronto, forged a bond of friendship.

On closer acquaintance the reconditioned fridge, bought cheaply, proved not such a bargain. It emitted a weird, whirring sound all the time the current was running. We would pitch our voices above the background noise; then, with a shudder that vibrated through the tiny kitchen and on through the living-room, it would cut out suddenly, leaving us, in the ensuing silence, shouting at one another like Latins having an animated chat.

Part of the entertainment at Eva's and Ben's was provided by their knowledge of numerology, the science of numbers. Benjamin took it seriously, the rest of us less so, even when he wore his poker face. Our lives, he said, are governed from the cradle to the grave by numbers; we use expressions such as 'his days are numbered' or worse, 'his number is up'. We can put 'two and two together' unless things are 'all sixes and sevens' and he went on to explain how numbers work, what they mean.

Numerology is an ancient science, highly developed during Egyptian times. Each letter of the alphabet has a numerical value. There are nine primary numbers: A=1, B=2 . . . I=9, then back to J=1 and through the alphabet to Z which is 8. Using this scheme, to find the numerical value of a person's name substitute a figure for a letter; the figures are totalled across, then reduced to a single digit, eg: 29 becomes 11 which is reduced to 2; 30 is 3; 41 equals 5. The birth date is added up and brought to a single figure in the same way. Each primary number carries particular qualities, a bit like the signs of the zodiac, only Ben made it seem much more complicated (after all it is a science!) because although the final number arrived at is important, its constituent parts, he said, are also influential. Where obsessive readers in the absence of any other reading matter might scrutinise sauce bottle labels, Ben and Eva were hooked on numbers. First there was the date – was it going to be a good day or not? Then there were car registration numbers, but we hadn't got cars, therefore street-cars had to suffice, street-car tickets, telephone, house or apartment numbers . . . The unlucky number was not thirteen but eleven or figures from which eleven was derived, eg: 38, 74 or because this was Canada, where house numbers go on for ever, 5321 . . .

Ben worked out our guiding numbers, the result showing that Jeff and I were compatible, which was what we had already decided for ourselves. Still, in an uncertain world, it was reassuring. Blanche and Roy also fared favourably; but his own and Eva's numbers were in conflict – probably because they were married longer, we thought, but didn't dare say it.

I have always loved Christmas, the preparations, carols, food, family gatherings, Midnight Mass . . . but that year in Toronto I could not engender any enthusiasm; by the middle of December, when the frenetic activity surrounding our arrival had abated somewhat, I was overwhelmed by homesickness and a longing for my family until I was feeling very sorry for myself. Jeff must have found my moping tiresome, but he never complained. I think, in general, women after marrying remain more in touch with their families than men do. The saying: 'A daughter's a daughter for all of her life, but a son is a son till he marries a wife' has a good deal of truth in it. In Jeff's case, even if he had not married me, he would very likely have gone abroad anyway. And, it is not part of his nature ever to look back in regret. 'Maybe . . . ' or, 'if only . . . ' have no place in his vocabulary. He makes considered decisions then takes whatever action is necessary, promptly. For instance, he was very cross indeed at the way the emigration in London had misrepresented the availability of employment in Toronto, persuading us to arrive on the job market in winter rather than during the following spring, as we had wanted to do, but now that we were here, he didn't waste any energy bemoaning the situation. To find work quickly was imperative, so, he tramped the streets until he found some. It was the same with his previous life − he had enjoyed it, but that had been bidden good-bye; his sights were now focused on the future, our future. He was a self-reliant, self-contained person.

Down-town, there were coloured lights, with the store windows suitably dressed for the occasion, but how different it was from London and Dublin. My boss questioned me about Christmas in Europe; then inquired, "Have you seen the decorations in Yonge Street?" On replying that I had, he continued enthusiastically, "Aint they jus' marvellous?"

There was a momentary pause while I choked down the remarks, which trembled on my lips, before stuttering lamely, "Yes . . . yes." How could I tell him what I *really* thought of Toronto, that the decorations, such as they were, were garish? In fairness, I should mention that 'marvellous' in Canadian English was not a superlative but meant simply: nice. Like much else that has changed for the better in the city so, too, have the Christmas decorations. Nowadays, it is a thrilling place to be (when suitably attired!) especially after dark, but Toronto's new City Hall − two curved towers of differing height − fronted by Nathan Philips Square with its lake, fountains, floral gardens in summer, transformed in winter to a fairyland with one hundred thousand lights and floodlit outdoor ice-skating, was for the future.

But what Toronto lacked, all those years ago, in sophistication, it made up for in efficiency, convenience, comfort, commonsense . . . I worked in the offices of heating oil suppliers. They operated what they called 'A degree day system'. For each customer's premises a record was kept of the indoor thermostat setting as well as oil consumption per degree of outdoor cold. In the office, outdoor temperature plus wind chill charts were kept daily, making it possible to assess how much oil remained in each dweller's tank. Deliveries were then made when necessary. Access to oil tanks, also to gas and electric meters, was possible from the outside of buildings. None of this poking around cubby holes armed with a torch, as meter readers still do today in many homes in Britain.

My moaning about the indoor heat in Toronto would have been matched by complaints about the cold had I been wintering in Dublin or London, because few private houses there had central heating and the privileged ones that had, usually relied on solid fuel. For most, a coal, gas, or electric fire in the living-rooms was the extent of comfort available. The bedrooms were often cold enough for frost patterns on the *inside* of windows on winter mornings!

Washing machines were commonplace in British and Irish homes, but dryers, refrigerators, freezers, dishwashers and suchlike were the exception rather than the norm, as they were in Canada. On the other hand household furniture, carpets and furnishings were far superior back home. The ubiquitous three piece suite was replaced by a two piece: a settee and *one* chair.

Practically all houses in Canada have a basement. In some it is just an open space; in others it is divided into rooms, utility room, store-room, work-room, extra bedroom or bathroom and, in homes with children, a playroom or 'rumpus' room. Invariably, the basement contains the central heating boiler, also the washing machine or laundry-room. We were told, in those days before air-conditioning was commonplace, that it was a favourite place to sleep during the hot, sticky, summer nights, which Toronto would get for weeks on end. In the bone-chilling season, we found it difficult to give credence to that weather forecast!

The office where I worked was situated in the basement of a down-town building. The decor left much to be desired, well, to be truthful: almost everything to be desired. It was pleasantly warm. It wouldn't have been a good advertisement for the firm if it were otherwise, would it? There was little natural light, only glaring fluourescent, which did nothing to beautify the linoleum-covered floors and drab paintwork, but the staff were extremely friendly and welcoming.

Apart from the Suez crisis, there were also reports in the media about IRA activity in Northern Ireland (what's new?) and they expressed surprise that I was no better informed on either issue than they were. Did they think that, because we had been nearer geographically to these places, we would have had some inside information! For their part, they were appalled at the atrocities committed by the Ku-Klux Klan in the USA. In Ontario there were few black or Asian people then and there was little racial disharmony.

A few days before Christmas there was an office, daytime party. How different it was from the grand affair with champagne in the oak-panelled office in London's Pall Mall, where anyone in a senior position to one's own was addressed by surname. Now, many have adopted the North American custom of calling people by first name often from first meeting, but newly-arrived from the British Isles, we found the familiarity disconcerting; at times confusing, for how could we differentiate between Pete the janitor and Pete the boss? Often we didn't know surnames: all part of the lack of permanency in contrast to the stability of life-style we were accustomed to.

But to return to the party, first names only did make for a very relaxed atmosphere and I met many members of staff whom I had not known previously. There was an attractive, young Canadian woman, who had resided in London for several years, before she and her English husband and child had come to Toronto. Her husband did not like Canada at all and he returned with their son to England. She did not wish to make a home there, therefore, they lived separately, and had done so for seven years, at a distance of three thousand miles, the Atlantic Ocean between them. She was looking forward to their visit at Christmas.

There was the expected abundance of food and beverages, mostly alcoholic! It was the first time I had seen glasses of 'rye (or Scotch) on the rocks' — neat whisky poured over ice cubes — and even many females didn't give the ice much time to melt, as a result proceedings got very jolly early on. I was astounded by the variety of fripperies and disposable products. It was a throw-away society: a couple of days later the Christmas trees, even the artificial ones, with all their trappings, would be flung out with the garbage. Boxing Day was not a general holiday (it did not become a paid holiday until 1989). Jeff would have just one day off, but we, at the office, could take two days: 24th and 25th or 25th and 26th; I chose the first; then it would be back to normal, Christmas forgotten.

Blanche and Roy were going to New York. We arranged to spend the day with Eva and Ben. Some firms gave staff a present of a turkey; luckily I got one (the others did not) because I doubt if we could have afforded one otherwise. Eva was to have the honour of cooking it. The middle tier of our wedding cake with some alteration of decoration became a Christmas cake.

On Christmas Eve we attended Midnight Mass with another couple from Dublin, whom we had got to know, returning afterwards to their apartment, quite luxurious, but they had been in Canada for two years; we took heart that some day we could live in similar fashion. We talked and talked as Irish folk are wont to do then, in the bitterly cold dawn, we were driven home in their big, fast car. After a few hours sleep we went to church again en route to Eva's and Ben's, where on arrival we got a great welcome. With imagination but precious little money they had transformed the living-room; there was a real Christmas tree for the children; decorated with baubles, tinsel streamers and an enormous bow of red crepe paper in its centre to disguise the lack of greenery, because of which Ben had bought it for next-to-nothing.

Dinner was served. We duly acknowledged the skill with which Eva had overcome the limitations of her kitchen. How she got anything, let alone a large turkey, to cook properly in the temperamental oven of the iron gas stove was near miraculous. The Big Black Monster, our name for it, was placed just inside the archway leading from the living-room. Perched on four squat legs with three gas jets of varying efficiency, or inefficiency depending on the gas pressure, with a broken plate-rack overhead and a badly chipped enamel splashback it took up most of one wall, dominating the box-like room. The oven door, which did not fit correctly sported a broken handle. There was a loose floorboard and any time you forgot to tiptoe reverently past the stove, the floor would sag and with a loud clatter, displaying annoyance, the door would drop off. Eva became expert at grabbing it — in midfall, so to speak — hitching it back into place, giving it a resounding kick for good measure. The stove would scowl back at her.

It was a good meal. Afterwards we chatted about our life in Toronto and what the future might hold for us — our present employment held little prospect. We scanned the jobs on offer in the newspapers (not that the columns were long) which had accumulated during the week.

"Here's a great job," Ben crowed. "For you and me, Jeff, because there's more than one."

The employment in Atomic Energy promised opportunities with excellent remuneration, in a place called Blind River. None of us had the foggiest idea where that was, but we gathered the settlement was godforsaken, because the advertisement explained that housing accommodation was being built 'so that wives and children would soon be able to join the men folk'.

Having discussed that we could save a fortune by living there for a period, before returning to civilisation: prosperous, Jeff and Ben decided that they had better send off applications for the jobs pronto. Their letters had to be carefully worded. Nothing that might enhance their chance of success could be omitted, but neither should the applications be long-winded. After many attempts, accompanied by much raucous laughter, they were finished, stamped, and in a surge of enthusiasm Ben went out there and then to post them. I might add that they never received a reply, but when we found out where Blind River was, none of us was sorry, though the cash would have been nice!

That was how we spent Christmas Day. A festival with a difference?

## Chapter Five

"I've been sacked," Jeff croaked in a barely audible whisper as he sat heavily on a chair, still wearing his outdoor clothes — minus his shoes, of course.

It was the Saturday after Christmas. I was preparing lunch in the steamy kitchen when he came in.

"Sacked!" I echoed. "Whatever for?" I asked bewildered, naively thinking sacking was reserved for misdemeanours.

"Nothing . . . just they're slack . . . last in first laid off . . . paid me up to date . . . that's it."

"No . . . no week's notice . . . or . . . or anything?" I stammered.

"No. No week's notice."

Until then, we had not realised that in Toronto you could be booted out without warning. It embraced many types of employment. Used to life where the ordinary working person enjoyed job security, this was an unexpected calamity. Even in the 1980s when hundreds of thousands in the UK lost their jobs they had some measure of protection, some preparation for redundancy and not the instantaneous chop as in Canada. It was the very worst time of the year to be jobless with the likelihood of remaining that way for months, until spring. There was no Social Security nor anywhere we could go for information or help. We had slithered back to square one again.

Despite the fact that it gobbled up most of what was left of our capital, we had, in December, paid costly medical insurance premiums, prompted by advice from the natives of the possible dire consequences of not having cover. We felt the expense had been worthwhile when, a few days before

Christmas, there were reports of a child dying in an ambulance outside a hospital having been refused admission, while the authorities debated who was going to pay for her treatment, because she was not insured. On her death, no doubt, the row switched to who would pay for the ambulance. There was nothing for nothing in Toronto.

Needless to say, the recruiting officials had given no hint of the expense of medical insurance, emphasising once more how ludicrously inadequate our funds had been on arrival in Canada. Life's little setbacks never come singly, do they? I had been feeling unwell for a couple of weeks, secretly hoping I could take some time off; fat chance of that now!

We saw out the old year at Eva's and Ben's with Blanche and Roy, returned from New York, excited by the prospect of moving permanently to the USA thanks to Roy's having applied for residence there. Laughter was our safety valve. When we were all together it often bordered on the hysterical, but it enabled us to keep a sense of proportion; we drew strength from one another: 'Sweet are the uses of adversity'. Benjamin playing with numbers gave us forecasts for the future when we toasted the New Year hoping it would bring improvements all round.

By morning the outdoor world had been transformed, the night having delivered to the city the first heavy snowfall of the winter. There had been light snow showers intermittently for weeks, but this was the real thing. A waterfall of flakes tumbled earthwards past the window, where I stood remembering my Johannesburg friend's elation in London the year before, on seeing snow for the first time. "Snow! Isn't it simply wonderful!" she had exclaimed, excitedly. (But when it persisted for a whole week, she became less and less enthusiastic until she swore that, if she were lucky enough to survive the rigour of winter, there was no way she would stay in England to experience another one.) What would she make of this? Visually it was gorgeous. I acknowledged readily that the comfort we experienced everywhere in Canada made it easy to be appreciative of winter's beauty — even when the sky was overcast there was the brightness of the snow — while I was inside looking out; however, to be out there in the great outdoors remained reprehensible.

Some days later, I felt too ghastly to get out of bed. Jeff was going to hike around Toronto as he had been doing daily, looking for work — any sort of work. Winter had really got into her stride, the snow lying several feet deep. He was glad of his overshoes; he could not afford to spend much on fares, but with his fur hat at least his extremities were protected from frostbite.

Before leaving, he phoned the office to say I would not be in. Ella must have eavesdropped because a couple of knocks on the bedroom door heralded her arrival, waking me from a fitful doze. I thanked her and said that I was all right. She left me, but not in peace to sleep. Oh no! She chased the vacuum cleaner about the house for an age; not a speck of dust was permitted to linger undisturbed, anywhere. Then she polished and dusted, to the accompaniment of a radio playing loudly in the background, the dozens and dozens of gaudy knick-knacks, that adorned every horizontal surface. She had half a dozen different coloured sets of decorated towels to deck the bathroom and, though they never seemed to be used, these were changed twice weekly to match the toilet rolls. Keeping house for herself and Jim was a serious matter. I once heard him, spluttering with suppressed laughter, call, "Ella, Ella . . . come and see this on TV."

"I can't," she wailed, "I'm cleaning the sink."

Usually, I felt sorry for her. She had no children and she did not have a job or outside interests, therefore her home was her pride and joy, but on that occasion all I longed for was quiet.

In the late afternoon Jeff returned, frozen stiff, utterly despondent.

"There doesn't seem to be any work anywhere," he said flatly, dragging off his wet clothing, numbness making him awkward. He went on to explain that, earlier in the day, when he had been overcome by the cold, he had resorted to spending money on a meal in a café, not only because he was hungry, but to give him the opportunity to thaw out.

"How are *you?*"

"Not too bad," I answered with forced cheerfulness.

Now that we would have to exist on my weekly wage I

would have to go to work next day. It was a case of Hobson's Choice. However, feeling wretched, I decided that, whatever the cost, a visit to a doctor, which Eva had been urging for some time, was needed. There was a surgery – doctor's office in Canadian speak – nearby. In the evening I went there. My suspicions were confirmed. I was pregnant.

Stunned, without looking left or right, blindly I stumbled across the street, along the dark passageway, up the narrow steps to let myself in through the two doors – remembering in my agitated state to remove my boots – and all the time keeping a weather eye out for Ella. I thanked God fervently that she was not in sight. I could not have faced an inquisition. Undetected, quietly I mounted the stairs, into the kitchen, to Jeff sitting at the table scouring the newspaper. I nodded to the question in his eyes. A smile flitted across his face while he guided me to a chair, then stood hovering protectively. A great, black cloud of misery swamped me. I didn't realise I was crying until the tears, dropping off my chin, soaked the front of my blouse. Silent tears.

"Please darling, don't," he pleaded, his voice breaking, but quickly gaining control again, I could hear him soothingly assuring me that everything would be all right.

Ever the optimist, Jeff manages always to be positive. Where I see something half-empty or half-done, he sees it half-full or half-completed; but I was too dejected to be cheered up. All I was aware of was reality in all its starkness: our savings had gone . . . we had nowhere to go for help . . . Jeff was jobless . . . I would only get paid if I went to work . . . I felt ill. The proverbial final straw fell, with all the weight of an iron girder, when we discovered on reading our medical insurance policies that, to qualify for maternity expenses of any kind, premiums would have to have been paid for ten months prior to the expected date of birth; unless my pregnancy defied all the laws of nature, we would not be making a claim. There was no way Jeff's positive thinking could influence *that*. The qualifying conditions were as definite as pregnancy itself. There are no degrees of pregnancy . . . no one can be mildly . . . slightly . . . more pregnant . . . It is one of life's absolutes.

Next day, and every day, I did go to the office. 'There is

nothing either good or bad but thinking makes it so.' No, not Jeff being philosophical, Shakespeare this time. While I agree with the Bard that one's mental attitude when confronting difficulties is important, no amount of telling myself I was imagining my morning sickness was any deterrent as I vomited repeatedly, making it necessary to rise earlier and earlier to get to work on time.

Bumper falls of snow alternated with heavy frosts; soon we were living in a giant, white ice cube. The appalling conditions were the worst for a decade; Canadians, themselves, were grumbling. On January 15th the temperature dipped to an all-time low for that month and this record remained until 1994, when again, Toronto experienced a worse-than-usual winter.

Each morning after several bouts of vomiting I trudged to the corner to jostle in the queue. Usually snow-ploughs succeeded in keeping the roads clear by shoving the white stuff into great banks along the kerbsides, leaving gaps here and there through which pedestrians scrambled to board the odd street-car that stopped; most clanged past ram-jammed full. Sometimes fresh falls of snow negated the job done earlier by the ploughs; then the ever-lengthening line would stand watching vacantly the crazily spinning wheels of the motor vehicles, their tyres trying to make contact with the road – down there somewhere. But worst of all for us onlookers was when a plough passed, spraying us liberally before erecting an embankment leaving us trapped on the wrong side of it. When I did manage to get on a street-car, (these were normally linked in pairs at rush time) after much heaving reminiscent of the London underground, before long I would feel suffocated or worse and would have to fight my way off to be sick in a gutter, to finish the journey on foot. In a nightmare of nausea I would struggle through the day somehow; then the trek home, which took for ever, followed by a display of fake bonhomie in answer to Ella's greeting and up to the kitchen to Jeff, worn out from a fruitless day's tramping around Toronto.

We both got more jumpy each day. Our pokey, stuffy rooms began to get on our nerves. It was a small, open-plan house; Ella and Jim were always on site, always initiating conversations. It was friendliness on their part, but we found it intrusive. On our first day in the flat we had closed the hot air vents; despite that, the rooms were stifling because of the hothouse temperatures elsewhere. After much effort Jeff opened the casement windows about three inches, but in the kitchen we were thwarted by the storm window on the outside, which had only a row of small holes along its base. Anyway, our triumph was short-lived — the best things in life may be free, but not fresh air in our flat — Ella said the windows were causing a draught and requested us to shut them. We did. They froze up. We were unable to open them again.

The sink was also a bone of contention. Every morning without fail she waylaid me, while I was putting on my boots at the front door, to ask anxiously if I had remembered to scour the sink; and every morning I assured her with suitable gravity, that I had. She didn't like us having visitors — not that we had many — and those who did come were asked by us to remove their shoes, but on one occasion an insurance agent, very important-looking with leather brief-case and fur-collared coat, called to see us. He mounted the stairs fully shod. The toe of one of his shoes came into contact with the white paint and was seen by Ella, who was hovering in the hall. I didn't hear the end of it for a week. The mark on the stairs even took precedence over the cleanliness of our sink!

Worry gnawed us. No longer was Jeff confining himself to answering advertisements for vacancies in the city, but he was applying for work in places we could not find on our map. Eventually, for one such job he was accepted. It meant that within a month he would join a survey party heading north to God knows where for heaven knows how long. I would not be able to accompany him.

To escape the kitchen's migraine-inducing, psychedelic wallpaper, and the smell of cooking, which made me feel ill, we took to eating our meals off an ironing board in the bedroom. It seemed the opportune time to look for somewhere to live near Eva and Benjamin: I would need company when Jeff departed to work in the hinterland. Anyway, my pregnancy would soon have to be declared and Ella was not likely to suffer the squawk of a newborn . . . The thought of it would be enough to give her hysterics.

Canadians, we had observed, moved from one job to another with little or no notice, the breadwinner willing to live away from the family home when necessary. Ever eager to show how acclimatised we were becoming to life in our adopted country, we refrained from complaining too much about our pending separation.

With less trouble than we had anticipated we got a flat near High Park in a big house with a carved oak staircase lit by a stained glass window, at a rent similar to what we had been paying at Ella's. Though sparsely furnished, our upstairs rooms were pleasantly decorated. We had all the privacy we desired. A baby would be welcomed. We could turn the heat up. Turn the heat down. Open windows. Breathe. Walk upstairs in our outdoor shoes if we had wished, but by then we had adopted the Canadian custom of leaving mucky shoes or boots in the special tray by the front door, to change into house shoes. (On a recent, winter visit to St. Petersburg we were invited by Russians to a meal at their home. Jeff and I brought a change of shoes. Our hosts were pleased. By their apartment door was the customary shoe tray with slippers at the ready, just the same as in Canada.)

Before taking up residence at our new place, we had the indignity of having to abandon one of our trunks in the snow in the front garden, there to remove its contents and once empty, Jeff had to break it up and burn it. Why? Lou, our new landlord, said it had woodworm. They were ancient holes, antique Irish holes, which had long been deserted by their beetles, but no way was he allowing *that* over *his* threshold. The house had woodblock floors and a beautiful staircase, therefore we understood his concern; not that that prevented us cursing him sotto voce, while we trudged through the snow and upstairs, to and fro with all our belongings. Next day we went with him and his two children, Jan and Maya to church. Olga and baby Natalie remained at home. Like all Masses then it was in Latin, which we could follow, but how were we to know the half-hour homily would be in Lithuanian? We made sure to find an English church for the following Sunday.

Unexpectedly, Ben got promotion at Ferranti's, to a better job than washer-cutting; and Jeff got work with the same firm as a machine-setter-operator. He was in the guillotine shop — not decapitating anything, but setting cutters to cut copper bars (electrical). He missed cars, but this was varied work and it was better to be clean, warm and dry, than lying under vehicles, on an oily floor, in the cold. Better still, he would not be taking off into the wilds; we could remain together.

Our change of abode meant that I had a very long journey to the office and soon I felt utterly worn out. I would have to look for something else, nearer home. This might prove difficult, not only because jobs were scarce, but with my silhouette about to change, I would have to declare my circumstances. By a stroke of good fortune, I got work described as temporary, which I was told could last anything from a couple of weeks to six months. It was with a fund-raising agency. Several of us were taken on for a specific project. Not as far from home as the heating firm had been, this office, nevertheless, was a distance away.

Though winter had to be taken in small doses, we often spent a little time at weekends in High Park, nearby. The railings that had once encircled London's St. Paul's cathedral formed part of the enclosure of the rolling landscape of woods, a zoo, two lakes and several miles of roadway. Skaters, bundles of bright clothing, careered with abandon, iced breath going before them. Others, their boots making giant pock marks in the snow, struggled to haul toboggans to the top of slopes to slide swiftly to the bottom amid a powdery, white wash. Canada geese skittered along the shallow edges of a lake, splintering ice tinkling, or pattered gingerly further out.

Travelling was done now on foot to Eva's and Ben's. No more night street-car rides. Few people walked anywhere. Most Canadians had cars, which were used for journeys of even a couple of hundred yards. Subsequently, how often I heard the complaint from compatriots, "There're few places to go for a walk in Canada!" But in the depths of winter nobody in their right mind braved the elements to walk anywhere particularly after dark unless forced to by lack of transport. However, in retrospect — in other words the lapse of time playing tricks with memory, so that the good aspects are remembered more vividly than the unpleasant ones! — those brisk evening walks frequently gave us the opportunity to admire the splendour of the unpolluted heavens, a glory of vibrant stars; gardens with ghost-like fir trees; snow-enveloped shrubs like mysterious parcels; shimmering boles of birch, their branches silvered by frozen snow and frost-encrusted pavements glittering like jewelled ribbons. But . . . horribly cold!

One evening when we were at Eva's and Ben's, but Blanche and Roy were not, we got talking about psychic power. Eva claimed that everyone had this power — a kind of sixth sense — but in most it lay dormant through lack of use. I said I was quite happy not to exercise mine; I preferred not to anticipate the future, coping with the present was daunting enough.

"All right," she agreed. "I'll tell you about your past, using psychometry."

"Using what?" I gasped. It sounded much too clinical for comfort.

"Psychometry: the divination of facts about an object or its owner, from contact with that object," she went on, sounding like a dictionary.

What kind of a tree is a psychome-tree? I joked mentally. I was deeply cautious of psycho . . . anything.

"What does divination mean?" I asked.

"Insight or discovery . . . by holding an object, say, a piece of jewellery that is worn habitually, an expert in psychometry can give details concerning the owner of the object," she explained.

Calmly, Jeff said he thought *he* could do that. To my utter stupefaction he — whom I thought I knew so well! — proved that he could, when on taking Benjamin's watch in his hand, after a minute or two of meditative silence, he gave details of how he had acquired it with other particulars about his life that we hadn't learned through our conversations. They were very excited by this discovery. I less so!

Eva prevailed upon Jeff to do likewise for her. She removed

from her right hand the large, square sapphire and diamond ring she always wore.

"I'll just describe the 'pictures' I see," Jeff said quietly, his eyes closed, "because most of it is totally unfamiliar to me."

Flabbergasted, I listened with them while he related details concerning a group of young children surrounding a couple of adults, describing facial characteristics; clothing, including the children's fur hoods and muffs; buildings; cobblestones; even weather conditions and the fact that they were talking in a foreign language. He had spoken for seven or eight minutes, when the fridge burst into life making itself felt and heard, drowning his voice.

"Damn that racket," Ben said, bounding into the kitchen, disconnecting the offending steel hulk from the socket. All was quiet again. "What do you make of that?" Ben asked Eva, who was sitting immobile as though her mind was far away.

It was. Not only in distance, but in time, too. She did not respond immediately and when she did she spoke hesitantly, struggling to put her thoughts into words.

"That was my family home in Prague," she began . . . "I must have been about eight . . . my sister, a couple of years younger . . . almost thirty years ago." She paused, lost for some moments in reverie, before continuing slowly, "The cobbled yard was at the rear of our house . . . those men you described, Jeff, worked for my father . . . it's all coming back to me . . . " Another pause, then she explained, "There was a crowd of us children pestering them . . . I think we intended to go skating . . . ice-skating on a nearby pond . . . we wanted them to chaperone us. You've described it all so vividly, Jeff," she said, her eyes shining with unshed tears, "even the small details like the fur muffs. We loved skating in winter . . . I was a good skater then." She smiled briefly.

"Were you?" Ben interrupted, surprised, "well, here you can get plenty; better get some boots . . . "

"It's so accurate; it's quite incredible. I haven't thought about it for an age. You have great powers, Jeff," Eva said earnestly.

Then she proceeded to tell us of her life about which until then we had known nothing prior to her life in England. I think she was glad of the opportunity to discuss it. Speaking in her controlled way she said gently, "I was in Paris when it happened . . . that's why I am alive today."

When *it* happened? Jeff and I listened horrified while she explained how, apart from an uncle, who had survived mentally deranged, her entire Jewish family had been liquidated by the Nazis. She had been studying dress design in Paris when Czechoslovakia had been overrun and later went to England, married, but soon was widowed. After the war she made a visit to Prague where she succeeded in tracing her family's housekeeper, who told her that, one day when the family were having a meal, soldiers arrived without warning to round up Jews. Eva's mother had scooped up some silver teaspoons from the table; hastily removing her sapphire ring she surreptitiously handed them to the housekeeper with whispered instructions to keep them for Eva. The rifle-carrying men were getting impatient, nevertheless Eva's sixteen-year-old sister bravely had defied them by going to her bedroom, to return wearing her best hat; she then threw her arms around the housekeeper, kissing her good-bye, and with a broad smile, her head held high, she was herded into the waiting truck with the others. None was seen again. Those teaspoons and that lovely ring were the only momentoes Eva had of her family and homeland. She did not have a single photograph or letter. Nothing!

How right I had been to detect on our first meeting in the hostel kitchen, that her composure was born of suffering. She displayed no self-pity, no bitterness. It was evident that her sister's behaviour was a source of pride and strength for her. It was typical, too, that she should comment with admiration about the housekeeper's honesty in looking after the teaspoons and ring for several years.

Eva and Ben were very appreciative of Jeff's talent. I had not been clever in recognising it; thereafter I was less flippant about things psychic.

Canada was a safe haven for many who had fled the horrors of oppression. Presently she was offering a home to those escaping the Soviet tanks in Hungary. On hearing tales of heroism I felt ashamed at my own carping. My worries were insignificant in comparison with theirs.

The fiendish winter dragged on — likewise my pregnancy sickness and part street-car ride part walk to and from work. Despite the change to a nearer location, each day the journey home took anything up to an hour and a quarter depending on the distance I had endured aboard, before beating a hasty exit. Jeff was marvellously supportive during those miserable months. He shopped. He cooked. He helped with the cleaning and laundry. Often, anxiously, he suggested I should give up working, but his wage was insufficient to allow us to save anything and we would need equipment for the baby to say nothing about the huge fees to be paid in *advance* for medical attention.

Our letters home were carefully worded and not too explicit; we hoped they would not convey the worry and discomfort we experienced; instead, we dwelt on the positive — the potential Canada offered in return for hard work. We did believe, earnestly, that once spring arrived with more jobs available our anxieties would lessen. Between ourselves, with the luxury of hindsight, we regretted not having followed our own instincts about the folly of arriving in winter; we came into contact with others from home equally as disillusioned as we were, all wishing we hadn't been swayed by the emigration in London, who had claimed there were plenty of jobs. There were, not in the professions — a draughtsman Roy knew saw umpteen firms in a week without getting a job — but in labouring, which was seasonal work. Winter quite definitely was not *the* season! The emigration people had clearly not done their homework. Maybe it was not Canada they had in mind, there was, after all, great competition for new immigrants from Australia and New Zealand, too! Not that the correspondence from home was cheerful. The recession there was taking its toll showering financial difficulties on my family; and an aunt, a missionary returned from Africa, a lively, lovely person, died from cancer aged forty-two years. My homesickness was, at times, acute like my pregnancy nausea.

Ben had to take a couple of weeks off work when the cold affected the circulation in his legs and to keep some cash rolling in Eva managed to get a position designing, in a clothing factory. One evening when we were bemoaning the never-ending winter she asked Ben, "Was it like this in Vancouver?" (He had lived there for two years prior to marriage.)

"Heavens! No!" he replied. "We'd a terrific amount of rain but very little snow in the city; actually the winter was mild, more like Britain than Ontario. . . ."

"Let's all go to Vancouver before next winter," Eva enthused.

"Oh yes," I agreed, my usual cautious nature not giving the matter any consideration at all. It would be warmer outdoors, that was all I was interested in.

"We would need loads of cash," Jeff said. "Maybe we could get a firm to sponsor us if we did it as an advertising stunt."

At the time we were eating large, chocolate-covered biscuits called Wagon Wheels.

"I've got the very idea," Ben chortled. "We could go by horse-drawn covered wagons. Maybe the makers of these biscuits would back us financially."

The resulting laughter bucked us up. For the remainder of the evening Vancouver, on the Pacific coast of British Columbia, thousands of miles away, monopolised the conversation.

As the weeks passed, life slipped into a pattern and we became less ill-at-ease. Jeff is a very self-confident person, but I, at that time, struggled to overcome shyness. I was no longer crippled by it as I had been in earlier years, but it was still a handicap, and I found it extremely difficult to initiate a conversation; while to walk into a room full of strangers was sheer torture! We had expected all North Americans to be effusively outgoing like those south of the fortyninth parallel, in the USA, but we found Torontonians reserved; they seemed to be on the defensive when meeting someone from the 'Old Country' for the first time. Known then as the Dominion of Canada, their parliament was (and is) run on British, not American, lines. *God Save the Queen* was their anthem, the Red Ensign their flag; Britain was still regarded as the mother country; very different from today with its dual official languages: English and French (French only, signs in Quebec); Maple Leaf flag; *Oh Canada* often displacing *God Save the Queen* and above all its multi-racial, multi-cultural people, where each year English speakers of British extraction become a smaller percentage of the overall population.

On closer acquaintance, we found Canadians genuinely helpful and friendly, but never easy-going. If Canada was prosperous, it was the Canadian who had made it so. Current statistics at the time showed that it had the highest per capita productivity in the world. Extremely proud of their achievements, they were hard workers, mostly very tough; they had to be not only in physique, but also in mind, to face the severity of life in their country. They expected immigrants to be the same. What they were slow to understand was that, however eager newcomers were to settle down, it takes time to become adjusted to a new environment with a different scale of values, currency and for some (us for example!) a harsh climate. Their attitude was – you have come to begin a new life in *our* country, you are on your own from day one . . . it was *your* choice. We felt sorry for non-English speaking immigrants. Heaven knows we were finding it difficult enough to learn the ropes.

For some immigrants, though, the fierce winter weather was not unfamiliar. The owner-occupiers where we had our apartment, Lou and Olga, were Lithuanians, resident in Canada ten years. Their eldest child, Maya, had been born while they were at a refugee camp in central Europe, in midwinter, in a building open on one side to the elements; Olga described the snow lying deeply on the ground just a few feet from her bed when she gave birth. We had many enlightening discussions with them and their European friends. A regular visitor was a widow with two teenage boys, also Lithuanians. Accompanied by her two young boys and a girl of less than two years, this woman – and thousands of others – were marched hundreds of miles under the watchful eyes of militia. Several days after setting out, the little girl slipped from her exhausted mother's grasp to be swallowed by the crowd. When the distraught woman endeavoured to search for her, she was manhandled by soldiers, who forced her back into the line of tottering refugees to continue walking . . . walking. She never saw her toddler again, nor ever discovered what happened to her, or the child's father, who had been detained in Lithuania with all the menfolk. I marvelled that such people found the will not only to go on living, but to do it with such stoicism in a strange distant land. The unsung heroes of life.

Certainly they received no accolades for their bravery, because for the most part Canadians neither knew nor cared what had happened in Europe. We spoke to a man who told us that his city of Amsterdam had been liberated by Canadians, yet, on his arrival in Canada, he was dumbfounded to find nobody was the slightest bit interested and he was advised to forget the past. Today and tomorrow were far more important than yesterday. *Nobody* cared about yesterday. (In stark contrast modern Canadians place great importance on history and heritage. Who brought about the change in attitude?)

When they were not complaining about DPs, they fretted about 'our giant neighbour to the south', the USA, and they worried about the ownership and control of their vast mineral wealth and the commercial policies of American industries established in Canada, while at the same time striving to assert Canadian nationalism and their survival as an independent country. It was (and still is!) difficult to define what made a person a Canadian; the only thing that could be said with any certainty was that *not* wanting to be American was at the heart of being a Canadian!

## Chapter Six

"Because of Mavis . . . we'll have to go by the first week in June . . . at the latest." Eva was quite emphatic. I cannot remember which of us brought up the subject again of Vancouver; nor can I say when exactly discussions got under way, but it was probably in early February. Anyway, what had started as a joke, became a possibility until, whenever the four of us got together, we talked of little else.

Our first consideration was cash. What was the minimum sum needed to make the move to Western Canada? It was a distance of over three thousand miles; as far from Toronto in the opposite direction as Dublin or London! We agreed that thanks to misinformation, the difficulties we had encountered had been exacerbated by our arrival in Canada in winter with insufficient capital, when huge numbers of Europeans were streaming into the country. We did not wish to repeat this in Vancouver. There would be an influx of refugees there, too, but if we arrived in summer with adequate funds to help us to get established maybe we could make a go of it. How much cash was necessary? Ben estimated one thousand dollars for us because we would have to pay hospital and doctor's fees when our baby arrived; much the same for them.

"One thousand dollars, that's a fortune!" I exclaimed.

"And at the moment we haven't two dimes to jingle together," Jeff added, making sure we continued to live in the real world; his and my combined weekly salary at the time was less than a hundred and fifty dollars and here was Ben suggesting that we would need to save one thousand dollars in a matter of weeks! Was it because it appeared to be unattainable that we all readily accepted the challenge? Resoluteness, we liked to think, was our common characteristic; the more difficult the goal, the more we were determined to reach it. Resolute? Crazy was nearer the truth. Luckily, motherhood had bestowed some commonsense on Eva, hence her deadline of the beginning of June for our departure, its being, she said, the least risky time for me to travel, while also enabling us — we hoped! — to find suitable accommodation before our baby's arrival, scheduled for mid-August. We had fourteen weeks to plan the move and more importantly raise funds. Could we do it? We intended to try. Winter in Toronto had a purpose at last.

Because my salary was earmarked to pay for the coming baby, we endeavoured to live on what Jeff earned, but frequently we couldn't stretch the shoestring to make the ends meet; now it was clear that my salary alone was not going to yield sufficient cash in time; therefore we would also need to save some from Jeff's. Our efforts to achieve the near-impossible reminded me of a teacher, a nun, who had taught me. I never knew her to accept an excuse. No matter how legitimate, original or downright funny an excuse was, she just snapped in reply, "Where there's a will — there's a way," and with that retort the matter was closed. Now, years later, far from Dublin, I was often to think — with a little more respect than in the past! — of that nun's favourite expression. Certainly we had the will, but accumulating the cash presented a real challenge; there was no easy way.

Our budget, already wafer thin, would have to be whittled even further. Rent, food and travel to and from work became our only expenditures. Eva and I handed over our fortnightly pay cheques to our spouses and received in return our lunch money and car fare, for the following two weeks; not a dime extra; however, we did get satisfaction on realising that it was *our* cash which greatly contributed to our growing savings. Ben continued to roll his own cigarettes and Jeff refrained from buying a much-needed pair of shoes for work — they were not squandering money either! I greatly missed visits to the theatre, for years one of life's great pleasures; not that lack of money was our reason for non-attendance. Incredibly, there was no national theatre in Canada (outside Montreal) in the nineteen fifties apart from Stratford, Ontario, in the summer months, and the Winnipeg Ballet. We had been a couple of times to the Royal Alexandra Theatre in Toronto to see visiting companies, but the performances had fallen so far short of being riveting, that we were more aware of the faded glory of the plush and gilt of our surroundings, to say nothing of the excruciating draughts, than we were of what was going on on the stage. A dearth of cultural activities left a yawning gap in the lives of many Europeans, in this country: enormous, wealthy and interesting, but nevertheless a cultural desert, though Canadians were unaware of this aridity. There were no other convivial public meeting places; no pubs (not that I drink intoxicants) and about half a dozen licenced restaurants in the whole of Toronto. Folk did their socialising (and drinking) in their own houses; the alcohol having been bought in liquor or beer stores, their blank windows, like betting shops back home, giving them a furtive air. If they yearned for lively nightlife at weekends or holidays they went over the border to the USA. However, for us, this lack of entertainment was fine: it limited the temptation to spend cash.

At the supermarket, we exercised considerable restraint by buying only basics or goods on special offer. (Thrift learned then so influenced us that to this day we find it difficult to be extravagant.) The less popular cuts of meat were cheap. Lamb or chicken in a basket at give-away prices didn't contain the prime bits of the animal, but had plenty of nourishing meat nevertheless. I discovered a butcher's shop where liver was only nineteen cents a pound. Talking about this with Eva and Ben, they said they didn't like liver, but then agreed that, at *that* price, they would develop a penchant for it — and did! Food was inexpensive and plentiful and, apart from products made from flour, of good quality. But bread, cakes, biscuits (cookies) of any variety all tasted the same. — the same soft cotton-wool texture and horribly sweet. Airmail stamps cost fifteen cents, but prepaid airletters only ten; my young brother would have to forgo any more Canadian stamps for his friends.

Owing to its propinquity to the USA Toronto was a very Americanised city with many of its inhabitants more concerned with the amenities of life than with life itself. To have the current model refrigerator, washing machine or food mixer was of paramount importance to my married colleagues, while their husbands hankered after a new car each year.

Vancouver is closer to the US border than Toronto is, but it was not influenced by the proximity of numerous high-powered American cities; life out there, Ben assured us, would be slower, less civilised, if noise, speed, possessions and the rat-race necessary to procure them, is considered civilisation.

Although there were few of non-European origin (apart from Eskimos [Inuits] and Indians!) living in Canada then, in Ontario, the modern immigrant was regarded more as foe than friend. Daily, hundreds of Hungarians were arriving; most settled in the industrial belt of Southern Ontario. The average person was totally ignorant of what had happened in Hungary; Europe was a different continent; they had enough problems of their own.

"More DPs." (Displaced persons.)

"These Goddarn Hungarians coming here in winter, when we haven't enough jobs or homes for ourselves . . ."

They saw them as a threat to their financial security, because they accepted a lower rate of pay than Canadians demanded. For their part, many of the unfortunate newcomers suffered from severe culture shock plus the reality of finding only labouring work available, work Canadians themselves did not want, despite all their protestations to the contrary. Nothing was done at government level to educate Canadians (who were for the most part only first or second generation!) and immigrants to each other's needs.

We hoped this animosity would be less pronounced in British Columbia where, at that time, the racial extraction from the UK was seventy per cent. In Vancouver there was a large Chinese population but Western Canadians appeared to have learned to live peaceably with those of a different race. While we were making tentative plans for going west, Blanche and Roy were preparing to depart to live in New York, almost five hundred miles away. We had shared considerable fun in London and Toronto; it was sad to see them drift out

On board the *Empress of Britain*.

Some houses on Oakmount. There are seventy-five houses and no two are alike.

Setting out to cross Canada in our nine-year-old Dodge. Note how loaded the back is.

Lunch-time on the journey.

Lake Louise.

The Great Divide — British Columbia.
Jeff's 25th birthday.

The Kicking Horse River, Yoko National Park,
British Columbia.

of our lives, but promises were exchanged that we would keep in touch.

Ben decided a car was an absolute necessity, which, indeed, was true. Not being one to dilly dally once a decision had been made, he got a blue Chevrolet on hire purchase. Jeff and he could drive to work in style. Life was far from easy for them. Ben was still having circulatory problems, yet struggled to keep his job, while Jeff's work shoes were now held together by wire with no cash available to purchase a replacement pair, therefore we didn't begrudge them the comfort of their car ride.

Eva and I, travelling separately, were still dependent on swaying street-cars; well, they swayed when they moved at speed, which admittedly was not often, because they spent an inordinate amount of time at each intersection, where, up front, boarding passengers paid a set fare before pushing along the crowded vehicle. Toronto street-cars — single-decked like a tram — rival the London tube trains, or Italian buses, for number of bodies per square yard. The overflow slipped down the steps at the halfway exit door, causing the operator, when finally ready to move off, to bellow several times "off the steps" because the doors would not close until all steps were clear; the trespassing offenders would endeavour to find a toehold in the passageway clinging on to those nearby for balance. And so to the end of the next block, where the procedure was repeated. At times there was the added excitement of being brought to an abrupt halt between official stops, when the overhead trolley became dislodged. Out hopped the driver to put things to right. While stationary, the human cargo would expand again with several people ending up on the steps, then the scramble back into the passageway for the off. The journey was annoyingly slow. This, in a city otherwise very efficient, was surprising. Destination reached, shoulders, elbows and fists each played a part in the battle to alight. The medley of European languages spoken aboard confirmed that not many Canadians journeyed by this mode of transport. The street-car, if not a tower, maybe could be called a tube of Babel.

You may think that Bach's sublime hymn *Jesu, Joy of Man's Desiring* and me lying supine doing antenatal floor exercises in the kitchen do not have much in common, but for me the two are entwined inextricably. The hymn was the introductory music to a radio programme and, if I was not nearing the end of my early morning routine when the strains began, it meant I was behind schedule.

Eva had prevailed on me to join classes held on Saturday mornings in Women's College Hospital. There, a group of us, with bumps of varying sizes, was jollied along by an unmarried therapist of sylph-like proportions, who propounded Dick Grantly Reed's way to natural childbirth. Physical plus breathing exercises had to be practised daily with early morning being considered a good time. For me it wasn't! But nevertheless I persevered. (Certain operas also remind me of our time in Toronto. On Saturday afternoons a live performance relayed on radio from The Metropolitan Opera House in New York with interviews conducted by Rupert Bing in the intervals, provided much-craved entertainment.)

Exercises finished, quick breakfast, tidy up and out to do battle to get to work. Owners were responsible for clearing snow and ice from pavements (sidewalks) adjoining their premises — a chore which we, mere tenants, were glad to evade — but the snow disregarded this bylaw, falling at inconvenient times, obliterating the shovelling done earlier. Dashing for a street-car I often skidded ending up in a heap on the ground. Junior continued none the worse for these trip-ups.

If steam was rising from Lake Ontario it gave an indication of the temperature: at minus twenty or thereabouts the steam was visible because the lake was warmer than land. Steam or not I was glad to *see* the lake; it meant I was still aboard the street-car when I neared the office, instead of having abandoned it to finish the journey on foot.

My boss was a lady, a typical serious-minded, hard-working Canadian. She was fair in her dealings with the staff, showing no favouritism and none of the petty jealousies that, in the days before the women's liberation movement, men claimed women resorted to, once given jobs of responsibility. A tireless worker, she expected everyone else to be the same, always. Like many Canadians her attitude was: you are here to work; you get paid for that work: you work; if you feel ill or are unable to stand the strain then stay at home. All true! But . . . I couldn't afford to stay at home and in the office I didn't find it easy to keep slipping to the loo to be sick.

On first going there I had found her pleasant, but by no means as friendly as the rest of the staff. After a couple of weeks, I detected a change in her attitude towards me, as though she was making amends for her previous coolness. Her secretary explained, "You see she thought you were English; you are fair; you have a neutral accent; she dislikes English people, because she thinks they are condescending or supercilious, but you're from Dublin, that's different!" (At that time, a great many Torontonians were of Scots/Ulster extraction and appeared, at least superficially, not to have a great fondness for the English/British.) I was amused by this, especially as, personally, I had encountered, on several occasions in London, a definite anti-Irish bias. So much for prejudice!

We did not have facilities for preparing food or drinks, instead we took it in turns to go to a café across the street with our order, which would be sent over at breaks and lunch-time. There was one male typist, Bob, whose surname I never knew. He had an ageless cherub face atop a roly poly body. Food was his god. He chewed constantly. When approached by whomever was writing the order list, he would stop typing, tip his chair on to its back legs, balancing himself by gripping his desk with his chubby hands, close his baby blue eyes and with a smile of anticipation, contemplate what filling he would have in his sandwich.

"Not ham, I had that this morning . . . not salmon, I had that yesterday, not salad . . . not cheese . . . not . . . ah!" His smile would grow wider, his eyes open again, and with a clatter he would bring his chair back on all four legs: he had made his momentous decision.

"I'll have chicken," he would announce triumphantly, "on rye bread, with dressing . . . not mustard."

Then he would add in an earnest tone: "Don't forget, Real Fresh Bread."

No matter what type of sandwich he wanted, three times a

day he finished his order with the same words. Needless to say his nickname, unknown to him, was RFB.

Apart from that mild diversion, life was uneventful except when there were arguments about open or closed windows. Those in favour of them shut usually won. Without air-conditioning and with the heating going full belt, the atmosphere soon became a smokey blue haze (Canadians were less fanatically anti-smoking then) which was enervating. Once after struggling for some time to keep my eyes open before conceding that I was losing the fight, I approached our lady boss to ask if I could go home, because I could not keep awake. Startled by my bizarre request she readily agreed. I quickly departed in case she changed her mind.

One afternoon, home early from the office for a doctor's appointment, I went with Eva to collect Sara from school. We crossed the playground walled on two sides by snow. A reek of furniture polish, food and footwear hit us on pushing through the double doors, passing from the invigorating freshness outside to the stuffiness within. Down both sides of the long corridor at waist level pegs bulged with clothing. Stray scarves, odd gloves, boots . . . lay, amid pools of oozy mud, higgledy-piggledy underneath. A bell rang loudly. Now here, now there a door burst open releasing children like puppies off a leash. Noisy. Vocal.

What a palaver it was attiring bodies to brave the elements, even if only sprinting to a waiting car. First indoor shoes were kicked off, their owners hopping about in socks in the slush carried in by adults as they scrabbled for leggings, then boots. Little ones asserting independence, "I can do it by my own," proudly stuffing legs into wellingtons the wrong way around, which necessitated flopping onto their bottoms in the struggle to remove them again. Now tail ends were damp as well as feet. Others, dressing out of sequence, unable to get their shod feet into waterproof trousers, or don salopettes over snow jackets wailed while devesting to start from the beginning. When finally encased, arms sticking out awkwardly, eyes popping over a yashmak of scarves that threatened to throttle the owner, legs stiff, weighted by boots, helping hands were needed to put on their backpacks or satchels, bulging with house shoes, empty sandwich boxes, flasks (school dinners were not provided), then the padded creatures waddled out of the building like multi-coloured penguins.

Our first excursion of any distance in Eva's and Ben's car was to Collingwood, in the Blue Mountains, the highest point for skiers in Southern Ontario, which is otherwise mostly flat. Skiing was not on *our* agenda, though given different circumstances we might have been more enthusiastic for the Ontarion outdoors in winter; many of our friends and colleagues, including Blanche and Roy, were.

We drove the fifty miles to Collingwood through countryside beautified by winter and from the steps of a hostel, enormous dagger-like icicles fringing its eaves, we gazed in awesome wonder out over frozen Wasaga Bay shimmering under an azure sky. The Arctic cold was too severe for twenty-one month Jamie to venture outside; not that any of us was attired to withstand the stabbing wind scudding across the northern wastes. We soon retreated indoors for hot soup, followed by blueberry muffins and coffee, the need for sustenance taking precedence over admiration of our surroundings. We didn't tarry for long. With two children on board we needed to get back to Toronto before dark. Weather forecasts were always followed by reminders to car travellers to carry chains, also provisions, thermos flasks with hot drinks, sleeping bags, because hypothermia could, in a short time, claim victims in the event of a breakdown.

Here and there on our journey we noted markers or flags protruding from the snow, lonely indicators of entrances to farms or isolated houses, their gateposts long since buried by snowdrifts. A skein of geese streaked across the sky. The sun as it slipped to the horizon threw amber fingers of light over the hushed frost-stiff countryside. Trees made an intricate tracery of black lines against the honey glow of the heavens. Even the children had long since fallen silent. Snugly tucked into a corner back seat I had to concede that winter in Ontario, visually, was stupendous.

Ben had a phrase, "The time is not ripe," meaning it was not the opportune time to get involved in something. Though we had noticed they were no longer bubbling with ideas for the proposed move to Vancouver, we were, nevertheless, unprepared for Eva hesitantly stuttering, one evening, "Don't you think maybe we are too ambitious? Let's postpone the trip for another few months, better still leave it till next year?"

Jeff and I were too stunned to reply.

"Sorry folks," Ben rushed on, apologetic, embarrassed, "but we honestly feel *we* shouldn't make the move just yet. Can't put my finger on the reason why we feel this way. Let's say I know the time isn't ripe."

There followed discussion and counter-discussion each time we met. First they would be as enthusiastic as ever, looking forward to going out west; next they would be quite adamant that they were staying in Toronto until financially better off. "Don't look so miserable. It's only a postponement."

We, ourselves, still wanted very much to go, but spent a couple of weeks on a see-saw of optimism and doubt until one evening we said, "Well, we'll just go along on our own."

Now Eva was distressed. "It's all my fault for suggesting it in the first place. Mavis, don't go until after you've had the baby."

Jeff and I talked it over at length. Junior would cost much of the cash we had. I did not intend to return to work afterwards; so there would be no future savings. More adequate accommodation would be needed. We couldn't go on living on a shoestring any longer. Another winter in Toronto would mean buying suitable clothing; our precious baby would be cooped up (like many young children) indoors for months on end . . . We arrived at the choice facing us: either we went at the end of May, or put it off indefinitely.

"It's now or never," we explained.

We knew the possible disadvantages of going it alone, the risks involved; above all we knew we would miss their friendship, but in our heart of hearts we thought we were doing the right thing for us.

"Let's leave it to fate," Jeff suggested, positive, as always, "and if anything, however small, crops up to spoil our plans we'll take it as an indication that we should not go."

"OK fine," I agreed. Mentally, I respected his powers of clairvoyance. If he could see the past, why not the future, I reasoned to myself? He never referred to his being able to know either and, except for a few times with Eva and Ben, never exercised his powers, but, amazed at learning about his psychic sense, I thought it was possible that possessing this ability was one of the reasons why he seldom had any self doubts once he had made up his mind about something.

We considered the various ways by which we could get to Vancouver. Not by plane because that would just be exchanging one city for another without seeing anything in between. By train, was appealing. It would enable us to see some of Canada en route, but it would be expensive and we had a lot of baggage. Why not buy a car? It would take a hunk of our savings, but we could resell it in Vancouver, where, we were told, motors cost more.

Eva, seeing that we were in earnest about leaving Toronto, pleaded, "Give up the idea of going through Canada, go through the States. The roads are good there."

"Won't be anything to look at just wide turnpikes. We want to see Canada's scenery."

"Listen folks," Ben intervened, "you'll not see much of anything from the bottom of a ditch!"

"Anyway we have Irish passports; we haven't visas for the States."

"It won't take long to get visas . . ."

My temporary job showed no signs of finishing; I enjoyed the work and the cheerful atmosphere in the office. One of my colleagues, much older than I, was an English woman, from London, who had lived in Toronto for many years. She travelled extensively with her husband on business both in America and Europe and could indulge her interest in art and architecture as well as the theatre and music in the various cities she visited. I enjoyed her company. She understood the cultural shock I experienced on arrival in Toronto! One evening when we were going to have to work late, she invited me to her home for a meal. Her residence was resplendent with oriental carpets, beautiful furniture, silver, antiques, paintings, mostly acquired on her travels: a veritable museum. I was in my element. Then it was time to eat. She took me through to the dining-room. Acres of shining mahogany table stretched before me, empty except for two place settings, one on each side at the far end of this very long table. My spirit had been well nourished by examining at close quarters all the wonders of her house, which is more than could be said for my stomach, because the meal consisted of weak tea, in a Georgian silver pot, two dainty slices of bread served on best china, of course, and a boiled egg! Served me right! Torontonians, all is forgiven, I thought; you may not be experts on art, but you are in the art of being hospitable; they are generous to a fault.

Each Saturday I looked forward to seeing my fellow-travellers-in-pregnancy at Women's College Hospital, for our exercise followed by relaxation sessions. Gradually, I began to feel better, and my appetite returned, but that brought its own problems: the medical staff were very weight-conscious. They said that there was to be 'no eating for two'. There wasn't much eating for one! After months when even the 'smell' of food made me nauseous, now the mere 'sight' of it seemed to contribute to a weight gain! I struggled to keep to the diet sheet I was given, but did not savour many of the dishes it contained nor did I consider that salad with a 'vinegar or lemon-based dressing' in place of mayonnaise was appetising. I couldn't believe it when I was reprimanded for eating too much fruit: "A lot of natural sugar, you know."

We even began to have a liking for Toronto and debated whether we should stay, but the thought that when winter finally departed it would be followed by a humid, sticky summer, which in turn would give way to bitter winter again, assured us that the west coast was the place to be, therefore we continued to save and plan our departure, but were ready to abandon the notion if any difficulties arose.

## Chapter Seven

"Going by *car!*" an office colleague shrieked when I gently broke the news that we were going west. "To *Vancouver?*"

"Yes."

"Reckon that's three thousand miles!" she exclaimed.

"I know."

"When you goin'?"

"In a few weeks."

"But you can't . . . "

"Why not?"

"You'll be over six months pregnant . . . too much of a risk."

Silence on my part.

"Why not fly? The air company'll take you before seven months, but not after."

Mumbled excuses from me.

"Well go by train then," she suggested helpfully. "It'll take about three or four days, but it's comfortable *and* you'll see something of Canada instead of going into the States."

More mumbles.

"You don't say! You reckon on goin' through *Canada*."

Pause.

"No kiddin'?"

"No kidding!"

"But," she retorted, "there aint any road. You can't ride from Ontario to Manitoba . . . not through Canada."

"Yes, you can," I replied, on the defensive, through Northern Ontario."

"On dirt road!"

"I know there's the odd bad patch," I answered lamely.

"The odd bad patch," she mimicked, "means miles and miles and *miles* of gravel road, right 'cross Canada. In Northern Ontario alone," she gabbled on, "there are *hundreds* of miles of rutted tracks. Nobody ever travels up *there* 'cept 'tween the mines. Journeys are made by plane. Don't try to drive through Ontario. You're crazy! Nuts! Anyway your doctor won't allow it," she said, calming down, as though that would put an end to our wild scheme.

There the matter rested for a few weeks.

Almost imperceptibly the weather became less bad, that is it thawed more frequently, but still gave us a fresh dumping of snow from time to time, usually overnight, a warning that winter wasn't over by a long chalk.

The flat overlooked the garden below; Canadians call that space a yard. It might be the size of a football pitch, beautifully landscaped with lawn, flowers, shrubs, trees, yet it's still called the back yard! Ours had large trees, both fir and deciduous, whose branches made delicate patterns against the snow-covered ground. When the weather warmed up a bit, black squirrels did trapeze acts on the overhead wires and the birds became active; there were few winged creatures during the bitter months except the ubiquitous Canada geese on the lakes. Now, the jays made their presence known. (Whenever I hear their squawk I think of Toronto.) There were hundreds of them. I was intrigued to learn that the brown bird with dark pink breast feathers, about the size of our blackbird, was an American robin. Not only is it different in size, but it is unlike our robin in not being solitary. I often saw as many as four hopping about together.

As the snows retreated, we made car journeys to places within a distance of about eighty miles. One aspect of Canada, which is difficult to convey to anyone, who has not travelled further afield than Western Europe, is the sheer enormity of the place. Ontario (there are nine other provinces and two northern territories in Canada) is *four* times the size of the British Isles. It stretches from the fortyninth parallel to the Arctic circle, hence a journey of eighty miles or thereabouts was but a mere hop around Toronto's back yard!

Southern Ontario is flat. Winter now on the run, by no

manipulation of the truth could the countryside be considered picturesque; apart from huge, truly magnificent trees that flourish abundantly, the province lacks attractive physical features and looks its best — dare I admit it! — draped in snow; but Jeff and I, planning to leave the place for ever, were glad of the opportunity to do some sightseeing, with Ben acting as chauffeur. He and Eva continued to coax us to postpone going to Vancouver and we agreed we would if circumstances spoiled our plans.

In the meantime we visited Owen Sound, Barrie, St. Jacobs, with its black-garbed Mennonite community: like people from a bygone age they quietly live out their lives ignoring the twentieth century's existence. Midland, with three miles distant its Martyrs' shrine: St. Marie among the Hurons, honouring hundreds of Huron Indians along with their Jesuit priests, who were murdered by Iroquois Indians in 1649. It was about the time Oliver Cromwell descended on Ireland to drive her natives 'to hell or to Connaught', because, though he didn't like their religion, he did like their land. But atrocities in our own century prove that Man's inhumanity to Man, alas! is not restricted to any era, location or race.

Time has not dimmed the memory of one of our first trips: to Niagara Falls, eighty-five miles from Toronto, on the border with the USA.

"Bring your passports," Ben had suggested, "and we'll go over to the States."

"We won't be allowed in. We've got Irish ones, but no visas for the US," we explained.

"Bring them anyway."

The Queen Elizabeth Way, the highway from Toronto to Niagara, ran through Hamilton, bristling with steel mills: the Canadian Pittsburg. The famed fruit orchards of the peninsula were still leafless, but on islands in partly-thawed stretches of water along the way there were fishing huts. We knew several people, men and *women*, who *enjoyed* ice-fishing at weekends. The uninitiated — myself for instance — can't understand how any pleasure can be derived from sitting immobile for hours on end outdoors, in all weathers, dangling a line in the hope of catching a fish; and, very often, having caught one, throwing it back in the water again; but to regard *ice*-fishing as anything but a punishment is beyond my comprehension.

Deafened, drenched by spray, we were duly awe-struck by the immensity of Niagara Falls — a boiling cauldron. The Horseshoe Falls alone measure an incredible half a mile around the rim with a drop of one hundred and sixty feet. Niagara means Thunderer of Waters. Thunder they do continuously. In past ages the Iroquois Indians worshipped them; in any age superlatives are inadequate to describe them. In the depths of winter some of the water is halted by ice; even now, on the last day of March, there were gigantic floes crashing about in the turbulent broth of the Niagara River.

We were returning to the car for a picnic lunch when I heard someone calling me by name. Who was it? A near-neighbour of my family in Dublin, who was now married and living in Southern Ontario. I had not known that he had emigrated to Canada. What a strange coincidence that we should have chosen to visit Niagara on the same day.

It is widely acknowledged that the full extent of the falls is better seen from the Canadian side, where thirty-five miles of superb parks stretch along the border affording a panoramic view of all the falls and the river. It is possible to don yellow oilskins and black rubber boots and descend to marvel at close quarters. After our snack we wanted to do this, but Ben had other ideas.

"Let's cross by the bridge into the States."

"Why bother, Ben, *we* won't be given entry."

"Oh come on . . . nothing ventured . . . "

"All right," we agreed reluctantly. We had come in his car.

Spanning the river, almost a mile long with a raised catwalk four feet wide down its centre, Rainbow Bridge links Canada with the USA.

"Canadian?" (They don't require documents.)

"British," answered Eva and Ben showing their passports. (At that time Brits didn't need visas.)

"And you, sir?"

If Jeff had been able to drawl convincingly, "From Tronna," we might have been flagged through; instead he handed over our passports knowing full well what the outcome would be.

"H'mm. No visas," grunted the official. "Will you step into the office please sir, ma'am."

We reported as requested; joined a queue. Spent the entire afternoon there to be told, "Sorry, you'll have to get visas in Toronto."

Because Ben and Eva had refused to go 'over' without us, during the long wait Eva had had to cope with a fractious toddler and bored ten-year-old cooped up in the stuffy car.

"You promised we could visit America," wailed Sara on learning that, because it was getting late, we were going to drive straight back home. Jamie promptly fell asleep, which meant he would not want to go to bed at his usual time; there was a strained silence on the part of the adults and Sara continued to grumble about life's injustices to young people. On arrival at our flat, Jeff fumed and ranted at me about a wasted day. I could understand his annoyance, but why vent his feelings at *me* — it was entirely Ben's fault and he had not said anything to him! Jeff's anger didn't subside for days. It was our first real ding-dong since getting married. It was also the first time that I fully understood what life would be like with a partner who was born under the third sign of the zodiac: Gemini, the twins. Unfortunately they do not seem to be *identical* twins! Over the years my experience has shown (and others, in similar circumstances, have confirmed this) that it's like being married to two persons. The shift from sunny to stormy can be instantaneous, but it is never quite so fast the other way around! I don't really believe in astrology, but . . . However, I never think of Niagara without also remembering the 'turbulent broth' of Jeff's fury. The Niagara frontier in the last century saw many battles between America and Canada, but in the twentieth it is referred to as 'a border of friendship'. Really?

"I'll tell you now," he said, when a few days had elapsed and the air between us was no longer charged with dynamite, "we are definitely *not* going through the States. I'm not taking time off at my expense to *waste* in that damned visa office."

So there it was!

Easter was late that year. When I had complained about the ghastly weather even in April, the girls in the office agreed it was awful, but said, "Cheer up, when winter does decide to leave us it does it quickly." On Monday with several snow showers it was miserably cold, yet by Good Friday of the same week the temperature had soared into the eighties. Winter had gone at last from Southern Ontario!

A stroke of luck, which indicated we were right in our determination not to postpone our plans, came when a colleague of Jeff's remarked, casually, that he was selling his car, a nine-year-old blue Dodge coupé, something out of the Ark by Canadian reckoning, but Jeff, pronouncing it mechanically very sound, decided to buy it and thought it was a bargain considering its good condition. He arranged to have an extra leaf put in the back springs, to enable us to cart our clobber across a continent, having already transported it across an ocean. With the car ready, our plans were complete; it was a case of remaining in Toronto to accumulate more cash, and to wait for the weather to improve in Northern Ontario. April and early May were considered tricky months for traversing the gravel roads up there, however by the end of May they should be passable.

Our respective parents wrote expressing anxiety about our proposed trip, suggesting we should delay travelling until after the baby was born. We replied saying that my doctor had agreed it would be all right to undertake the journey, but that, really, was only a half truth . . . or much less! The doctor, like so many others, had suggested going by train, but seeing I was determined to use the car advised me to stop for frequent rests and not to attempt to cover a great distance each day. No, he didn't refuse permission but . . . I did not tell him that we were going through Canada! When it was completed many years later, the Trans-Canada Highway, a truly remarkable feat of engineering, became the longest paved road in the world spanning a continent from the Atlantic Ocean to the Pacific Ocean; but that was for the future, now it was under construction. Anyone from Eastern Canada wishing to reach the Western Provinces travelled south and crossed into the USA to re-enter Canada at Winnipeg in Manitoba (midway across the country) or further west than that. The doctor, obviously, presumed we were planning to do the same.

By the way, he also presented me with a huge bill knowing that I had no medical cover, and that the 'expensive' part of the pregnancy had yet to come. It may seem strange, but it never occurred to us to dispute his charges or to scarper without paying at all, and it was hardly likely that he would ever track us down if we reached Vancouver!

My office colleagues rained a verbal attack on me when the time approached for me to bid them good-bye.

"Hey kid you're nuts!"

"Goddarn crazy."

"Hope you won't regret it."

"Honey don't go through Canada, you're taking an enormous risk."

"Mad Irish. Rebels!"

All this *did* have the effect, for a while, of undermining my confidence in our ability to succeed, but even if I had coaxed Jeff to get American visas there was no time. We had crossed the Rubicon. Thirty-odd years later, in Rimini's old town, I was reminded of this when I saw the stone tablet recording Julius Caesar's crossing. There was no monument erected to commemorate *our* decision and not a single word of approval or support! It is an indication of our belief in each other that we didn't capitulate. There was no point in worrying ourselves into a frenzy of apprehension; we did nothing to alter our plans, which right from the start had run smoothly, suggesting everything would be all right. Jeff's self-confidence was infectious.

Occasionally I made attempts at studying maps, but on viewing the huge, empty spaces, particularly adjoining our route through Northern Ontario, I only got down-hearted, anyway there was only *one* road, as everyone kept reminding us, therefore a map was unnecessary. Instead I occupied my spare time packing china, glass, and all the paraphernalia we had humped this far. Not all of it would fit in the car; we loaded our winter clothing, bedding, my horrid brown boots – yippee! – into one trunk. Eva would send it on to us when we had an address in Vancouver. Optimistic, what?

"Let's buy a movie camera to take film on the trip," I

suggested in a moment of uncharacteristic extravagance. We had little cash to spare but buy a camera and tripod we did. Neither of us had handled a ciné camera before. There was only time to experiment with one reel of film and without a light meter there was a lot of guess work in setting the dial. Was it dull or cloudy/sun or hazy or whatever? We collected the processed roll from Kodak the evening before we were due to leave.

Undeterred by the lack of a projector, Ben, a great believer in necessity being the mother of invention, produced a cot sheet, which he pinned to the wall; with the aid of a lens from an old camera and a table-lamp draped with a tea-towel, he proceeded to 'show' the film, passing it slowly from hand to hand. The resulting picture was small, fuzzy, jerky, at best: dim, often non-existent, where we had forgotten to remove the lens cap before shooting, and . . . upside-down! Convulsed with laughter Eva, Jeff and I on hands and knees, viewed it with our heads touching the floor.

"What's it like?" Ben kept asking, irritated by our jollity — his role as 'projectionist' was so involved it prevented him from looking at the 'screen'.

Actually none of us had much idea what it was like, but we were certain about one thing: Pathé Gazette need not fear any competition!

## Chapter Eight

Like an excited kid at Christmas, I watched Jeff squeeze the last of the cartons into the car. All we possessed, except the trunk at Eva's, was in that Dodge, which was so laden that, despite the extra springs, its rear end almost hugged the road.

Before breakfast, Ben had helped Jeff to load the heavy items. They removed the back seat, placed a trunk on the floor, packing the space between it and the front bench seat with boxes of various shapes, all carefully positioned for ballast, then put the seat resting on top. Ben trotted off home saying that he would see us later. We had something to eat. Afterwards, the lovely soprano voice of Renata Tabaldi issuing forth full belt from our radio, we tidied the flat, alternating with running downstairs to the car to pile in coats, camera gear, a large paper bag with two hats of mine, a carton of Coke and sundry articles that kept turning up long after we had first said, "That must be everything." The car was packed and the flat was empty of our belongings. At the door I paused momentarily. We had been very happy here, but no going back now . . .

It was a glorious morning. The maples, which lined the wide roadway, were breaking into leaf. Everywhere, in the parks, the gardens, the hedgerows there was the promise of renewal. New life. My new life was kicking the daylights out of me energetically, as if to say, "Get going!"

The older children tripped down the porch steps to us bearing gift-wrapped parcels, presents for our coming baby. Olga emerged with plump, five-months old Natalie in her arms; then they were hugging me, wishing good luck and weeping copiously all at the same time, while Lou pumped Jeff's hand. Possibly, for them, it stirred painful memories of earlier partings, in Europe, nevertheless, it was a touching send-off from people whom we had only known for a brief time. Blinking back tears, I waved until we turned at the end of the road.

We had coffee at Eva's. They walked us to our car; an awkward silence descended. Why did conversation elude us? Farewells are always the same: meanderings delivered in voices which seem to have lost their normal tone, interspersed with long pauses. I hate good-byes!

"Why can't we go too?" wailed Sara, when she, then Jamie, kissed us.

Ben and Eva exchanged quizzical glances; I almost expected them to say, "We're coming. Hang on while we get our coats . . ."

"We'll follow in a few months," they assured us. This promise forestalled my tears, but there was an unswallowable lump in my throat all the same. They had been wonderful friends. Their good humour coupled with Eva's advice had kept me buoyant through a difficult time.

"Au revoir. Good luck. Safe journey."

We were off! I opened the notebook, which Jeff had given me, saying, "There can't be many others daft enough to turn their backs on the only folk they know . . . to journey three thousand miles on bad roads, in a nine-year-old car, when over six months pregnant . . . See what you can record."

Saturday, May twenty-fifth, I wrote, remembering it was my Geordie grandmother's birthday; we had visited her before setting sail from England. She and my grandfather had had the pioneering spirit in their early lives. I felt sure *they* would not disapprove of our adventure.

We drove out of town passing familiar buildings on the way, past Loblaws the giant supermarket, with adjoining car park and children's playground, where we had shown considerable restraint buying only basics, all part of our savings drive, past the modern apartment blocks, whose rents had been way beyond our means, past St. Cecilia's church with its attractive spire. I was genuinely sorry to be bidding good-bye to Toronto; likewise the previous day I was sad on saying farewell to office colleagues, whose friendship I had valued and whose generosity with gifts had bordered on the embarrassing. Even Real Fresh Bread took time off from eating to wish me good luck and one old dear presented me with a collection of her poems all written in beautiful copperplate. It echoed what Irish friends of ours had said, "You hate this place, its austere down-town buildings, its self-assured people, the cold in winter, steamy heat in summer, all the foreign languages . . . then suddenly one day you say, "Why haven't I seen it before? To be sure 'tis a grand place!"

Yes, it was a grand place, though my change of mind from dislike to approval had been an imperceptible process. There would always be the unpleasant climate, but it was heartening to be departing knowing that the residents had accepted us. It was to be a quarter of a century before we saw Toronto again and then its people referred to it, not as Hogtown, but Metro.

"Are you going to spend all day dreaming?" Jeff's voice cut across my thoughts.

"Just thinking back over the last few months. It seems an age since we lived in London, doesn't it?"

"Yes, but next place, Vancouver!" As always, the future not the past was of importance to him.

The city was soon left behind. Highway 400, that wide band of grey asphalt stretching for miles across the uninspiring countryside north of Toronto, which we had travelled many times in Ben's car, became Route 11. On we sped. The snow had cleared now, but despite the sunshine, the landscape was lifeless.

I switched on the dashboard radio. If it occurred in a story or film, it would be considered contrived: a soprano was midway through the aria *One Fine Day*. The music swelled; my spirits took an upward turn and were carried along with it. Yes, it was good to be on the road. We felt a great sense of achievement at having saved the necessary cash in such a short time.

Many city-dwellers own holiday cottages in the Muskoka Lake district. They think nothing of travelling more than two hundred miles each way every weekend from spring to autumn — or fall, as they call it. We passed through the town of Bracebridge, which is centre of this famed lake area. We didn't see many of the lakes, but signposts along the way indicated the tracks leading to them. At intervals, in clearings in the forest, there were lay-bys with picnic tables under the trees; also pit toilets, refuse disposal bins and a huge stone fireplace. The first time we stopped, some months previously, at one of these spots with Eva and Ben, on deciding to light a fire, we were amazed to find a heap of logs with kindling in readiness beside the fireplace. Quickly recovering from his astonishment at this benevolence, Jeff quipped, "The rotters, they didn't leave any matches!"

Many cars travelling south had American licence plates. "Whatever are those black things tied to the front of that big Chevvy?" I asked.

"Those 'black things' are dead bears."

"Ugh! how horrible," I shivered.

"Obviously those Americans think differently; they have travelled hundreds of miles to hunt, to return triumphant with the bounty. How proud they will be of their black bear-skin rugs," Jeff went on, teasingly.

"Ugh!" I said again in disgust.

We passed several cars displaying the results of their shooting expeditions. One such car was parked in a lay-by where we stopped mid-afternoon. The sight of the prostrate bear put paid to any inclination we had for food. 'Ontario abounds in wildlife, everything from grouse to moose and bear: a paradise for the huntsman,' said the blurb in a guide book. For the huntsman maybe, but if that is really what paradise has on offer I'll opt for the other place! Further north we saw notices: 'Beware of Roaming Wild Beasts' with warnings not to venture far from the road unless armed.

Forests, a mixture of conifers and deciduous trees, gave way, from time to time, to rocky outcrops, pinky grey in colour. There were no further picnic pull-ins. The scenery became more attractive as we travelled northwards, with low wooded hills near the village of Huntsville. Birch trees were not yet in leaf, but some of the tamarack were greening. These northern forests consist of spruce, pine, fir, trembling aspen, white birch and tamarack, which is a type of larch.

Tall slender trees, they differ from all other Canadian conifers in that they are not evergreen. Trembling aspen is a poplar. It grows throughout Canada. Its smooth bark can be from pale green to grey to almost white; with leaves which seem to be perpetually in motion, the Indians call it 'noisy leaf'.

There were few signs of human existence until eighty miles further on a stone archway marked the entrance to the town of North Bay, often called The Gateway to the North. We knew only too well from all the advice we had been given that from here on it would become progressively more rugged. The easy part was over.

Nearby, is the town of Callander, birthplace of the Dionne quintuples; born in 1934, they were the first quins in the world, all girls, to survive into adulthood. I remembered how fascinated I had been on hearing about them and looking at pictures, when I was a child.

We booked into a small hotel offering accommodation only near Lake Nipissing. It was already well after 6 pm. We had supper and took a short stroll. Colourful chalets like doll's-houses were dotted among the trees on the lakeside. Evening sunshine slanted across the calm expanse of water – the lake is forty-eight miles long and about thirty across – spotlighting small boats, the sky giving no indication of the thunder which would crash about rousing us before dawn.

We attended early Mass in a dim church on the edge of town. North Bay is close to the Quebec border; the homily was given first in French, then English, which was an improvement on Lithuanian, or Ukranian, or Italian, with no English translation, as we had experienced before. When the collection plate passed, Jeff gave a dollar bill, the same as we did in Toronto. Such generosity was not usual here, apparently, because the collector, noisily, attempted to give him change! Years later, walking in a street in Wallasey (Cheshire), I was asked by a lady for directions to the nearest Catholic church. Commenting on her Canadian accent, I enquired where she was from.

"Ontario," she replied.
"What part?"
"Oh! a lil' place you wonta heard of, North Bay."

I told her I had been there.

"No," she drawled, "you must be mistaken . . . "

I described the Catholic church in the town.

"Well, what doya know!"

We agreed that, apart from Jeff, it was probable I was the only person in England who had been to Mass in her church. Of the thousands of people in Wallasey, why did she ask *me* the way? What do you know!

The storm came around again when we were getting into the car after breakfast at a café. It grew darker. Ominous rumbles in the distance died away only to return each time with greater force until the claps, of frightening ferocity, were overhead. Hailstones fell steadily, hissing in their descent to earth.

I bellowed above the drumming on the car roof, "I don't think this is the right road."

Jeff pulled up. "Let's see the map," he mouthed, his words lost in a deafening crash of thunder. "Where *are* the maps?" His face registered irritation at not being able to make himself heard.

"You had them last," I replied. "*You* were looking at them while waiting for breakfast, remember?"

Breathing heavily with annoyance, he reversed and drove back the six miles we had travelled, lightning zigzagging, the flashes following each other in quick succession. He dashed through the downpour, retrieved the maps and scuttled back to the car.

"Let's see," he said brushing away the rivulets of water, that coursed down his face. "North Bay? North Bay?" His finger found the town. "Here we are . . . then we turned . . . here, didn't we? U'm, yes . . . you're right it was the wrong road."

I don't know whether his surprise was at himself for being foolish in taking it, or at me for knowing that it *was* the wrong one. Now was not the time for anything but diplomatic silence.

Route 17 ran west from North Bay (ultimately, the direction we needed to travel if we were ever to get to Vancouver!), skirting Lake Nipissing and on for about two hundred and seventy-five miles, through Sudbury, Blind

River (of Christmas Day letter-writing fame) and on to Saute Ste. Marie, which is on a spit of land between the Great Lakes Huron and Superior, where Route 17 joined forces with a US highway in Michigan – we had no visas! There was no road in Ontario beyond that point; therefore, we would have to follow not Route 17 west but Route 11 *north* from North Bay, it being the only Canadian road through to Manitoba and beyond.

It gives some indication of the state of the highways that they were not more easily discernible from the local roads. Had we continued it would have petered out, but we would have had to return for the maps anyway – better sooner than later.

The sometimes red other times pink rock, with scattered trees gave way again to regimental woodland. Dark evergreens flanked the road on both sides, the towering giants growing so close to the edges, I thought it might suddenly end and we would be surrounded by them. But no! Slicing the forest in two, the road ran on mile after mile, an unbroken line until it merged into the distant horizon. At other times the highway was above the level of the trees and we looked over a sea of spruce, pine, fir, birch rolling east and west endlessly: a land untouched by man. Nothing but forests, rivers, lakes. Along the roadside the telegraph poles, the only link with civilisation, were encircled by high mounds of stones to protect them from the gusty blizzards of winter, despite that some of them stood aslant.

The vicious storm spent itself, but the rain continued with varying intensity for some hours. We were making good time when wham! The bonnet of the car wrenched itself loose to be flung up against the windscreen. Jeff slackened speed and stopped. No damage had been done. How quiet it was! Soundless. Creepy. The trees formed a canopy keeping out the light, making it impossible to see for more than a couple of yards into the forest. Remembering the warning signs we had read, at any moment we expected to see a bear crashing through the undergrowth. The Canadian black bear weighs between five and six hundred pounds and we knew that when they come out of hibernation they are ravenous . . .

The car's headlights pierced the dismal gloom; we drove on

for some hours passing through only three or four small villages on the way. Occasionally in clearings there were lakes; some with logs: massive tree trunks; others: great expanses of smooth, dark water, ominous, unfriendly. On progressing northwards these became more numerous. At times the forest gave way to flat, scrubby countryside, which gave no indication of the fabulous wealth beneath its floor: gold, silver, uranium and cobalt. The few hamlets marked on the map were clustered mainly around the mining area about two hundred miles north of North Bay, or hundreds of miles further on, near the grain-exporting, twin cities of Port Arthur/Fort William, but for more than *eight hundred miles* — the distance from London to Edinburgh and back — the highway ran through country almost devoid of settlements — no wonder our friends thought we were daft! There was the railway and our route (the Trans-Canada Highway); any other roads were only short stretches near the towns; otherwise the expanse of white paper, representing Ontario on our map, was splashed by a network of blue trails and blobs: rivers and lakes, suggesting that someone had gone berserk with a bottle of blue ink on a pristine, white sheet. It was easy to believe Canada's statistics: the world's second largest country possessing one fifth of the earth's fresh water. Ontario, of Iroquois origin, means beautiful lake. Aptly named. There are upwards of *half a million* lakes in the province.

The hitherto almost straight road became tortuous. The water in the river nearby was a peculiar greyish-green colour. We were nearing Cobalt with its silver mines. Within a few years of its discovery in 1903, it became one of the greatest silver producing centres in the world. Built on a hill on this winding road the town proved a disappointment with nothing about it to suggest the shimmer of silver or the blue of cobalt, but its name had fairytale origins. In German folklore a mischievous goblin, who haunts underground places, is called a kobold or nuisance; cobalt, in the early years of the mine, was considered bothersome to silver miners; later its value was realised with its use in jet engines, television equipment and in the treatment of cancer.

We pulled to the edge of the road (no picnic areas this

far north) to eat our lunch: sandwiches with hot soup and coffee in flasks, bought at breakfast time in the café. We noticed a small sign pointing east, indicating Kirkland Lake. Gold mines are located there. Eva and Ben were to move from Toronto to the town — not searching for gold, but to run a hostel for children. It was strange that in this vast area, partly swamp, partly wooded, we should choose that spot to picnic.

In the vicinity there is a village called Swastika. During the Second World War, it was suggested that the name should be changed. "Why?" the inhabitants demanded. "It's been ours longer than Hitler's. Let him get a new symbol."

The railroad ran close to the highway which was straight for many miles. The trains are infrequent — we saw none that day — but about four times a week one passes, carrying a few passengers and freight, everything except cars, all the goods needed in the small settlements it rumbles through. The railway was their life-line. We crossed a small river, which we discovered was called the Wicklow River. During childhood my holidays had been spent in Co. Wicklow, often referred to as the Garden of Ireland. How different from here where it was flat and barren with not a soul about! Shortly after 3 pm, six hours after leaving North Bay, we arrived in Cochrane, where we knew the highway swung westwards. Heading west at last! Until then we had been driving north from Toronto consequently, despite the mileage, we weren't getting any nearer Vancouver. There were *no* roads further north than this; the only land access is by railway. The hundred and eighty-six miles from Cochrane to Moosonee on James Bay can be made on a train nowadays, romantically named, the Polar Bear Express — it runs three or four times a week during the brief summer, and tourists can go along for the ride — but there were no such delights available for us, though a train did service the area. There are no settlements along its route, only isolated cabins about fifteen miles apart. Not only are there no stations, there are no platforms or steps. The train is stopped, as we would hail a taxi in a city street! Moosonee at the end of the line is one of the oldest settlements in the whole of Canada. Cree Indians there, from early times, were involved in the fur trade. What commodity is the source of their livelihood today?

There was a road sign. Not a big one. 'To the West' it said! We knew it was all of three thousand miles to the coast, but it didn't say that, just 'To the West'! We didn't really need the sign, the only road from here was going that way. This was the Canadian North: big and bleak and barren.

The hamlets were more sparsely scattered now. We passed through Smooth Rock Falls, home of Alitibi Power and Paper Company, where there was a famous newsprint plant, and on towards Kapuskasing. Before reaching it we booked into a motel, because there were none listed for the town. Cleverly, if not poetically, combining Canada's dual languages, it was called, Chez Ted's.

It was a long continuous building, not individual chalets. Each unit had its own parking space in front; we could keep an eye on the car, our mobile home, after all it possessed all our worldly wealth. A large, comfortable room served as a bed-sittingroom. Some motels had well-equipped kitchens; others, such as this one, had not, but there was always a diner nearby. Each unit had its own private shower or that's what we thought. Jeff was already deeply asleep in his bed, when I, having done some washing, switched off the light, to slip gratefully into mine. I savoured the cool sheets; it had been a long, tiring day. Drifting into another world, suddenly I was wide awake again. What was that? A sound from the direction of our bedroom/bathroom door? Burglars? But all was quiet, apart from my heart. Maybe I had dreamed it? No! There were voices. Men's voices.

"Gee whatja know, someone's goddarn washin', drippin'." The gruff voice went on, "Guess we'll have to do without showers." A loud click, a bolt being released, unmistakably our door, was followed by another one slamming. All was silent. I lay puzzling, then it dawned: it was a shared toilet/shower with the next unit. I rescued my washing and made sure to lock the door to the shower from our side. Jeff continued to snore blithely.

## Chapter Nine

Morning brought a deluge. Jeff, shoulders hunched, hands deep in trouser pockets irritatingly jingling coins, glowered at the window. I repacked.

"Come on. Let's get some breakfast," he said with forced cheerfulness.

It was unusual for him to be depressed. I felt uneasy. A blast of wind wrenched the door out of my hand flinging it against the wall of the motel, when we stepped outside. With needle-like jabs, the rain whipped at our faces. I grappled with the swinging door; banged it shut and locked it, while Jeff threw the case in the car boot; then hand in hand, heads bent against the driving rain we made a dash for the café's warm interior.

"Don't fancy hitch-hiking in this weather if anything should happen to the car."

He didn't put it into words, but I guessed what he was thinking: there would be little traffic; the possibility of getting a lift practically nil, and the road — one section in particular — could be treacherous in bad weather. How often we had been warned about it! Whenever well-meaning friends tried to persuade us to journey through the States, because of the good roads there, they would throw in a harrowing description of the alternative: The Stretch, if we attempted to travel through Ontario. Our breakfasts arrived and, because it would take much more than the mere *chance* of being stranded miles from civilisation to interfere with Jeff's robust appetite, he turned his attention to that; though I knew, despite his inherent optimism, he really was worried by what lay ahead.

We left the safety and warmth of the café. Within a couple of minutes, outside the town of Kapuskasing, the paved road ended, just like that! Despite my recent hot meal, there was a cold void in the pit of my stomach when the tyres crunched on gravel. Hundreds of miles of 'crunchiness' stretched ahead of us. I was scared. Very scared. Guilt-ridden. Too late now to acknowledge my foolhardiness.

A handful of houses dotted the flat bleakness. A school bus, a hideous shade of yellow, chugged along; children cluttered in rain gear and boots huddled in dismal groups by the roadside awaiting its arrival. When, some miles further on, we saw the school it seemed but a glorified shack. The road ran close to the rail-track. A train clunked by. The carriage windows blurred by snow and ice, the coachwork heavily mud-spattered, more goods than passengers aboard, it lumbered on its way. A lorry approached from the opposite direction; as it passed we spoke simultaneously, "That was covered in snow."

The dense forests of spruce and pine gradually thinned and then were left behind; here, the scattered, stunted trees were not yet in bud, the undergrowth and scrubby bushes lifeless. It would be June in a few days, yet winter was reluctant to let go its grasp. We were just south of the tree line, vegetation was scanty. Temperatures, in winter, of minus forty with lots of wind are common in the Ontarian bush. I could think of nothing intelligent to say and I knew that inane chatter would convey to Jeff the nervousness I was feeling, which would only accentuate his own misgivings. For his sake I tried to sit, if not comfortably, at least quietly. The car was warm.

Piles of sodden logs lay in heaps along the roadside. Nearing the hamlet, Opasatika, we ran into snow. Small houses built on tall stilts — to keep the living quarters above the winter snow level — had flights of wooden steps giving access; doors were narrow; tiny windows high in the walls.

The snow falling thickly cut visibility to a few yards. I had dreaded the 'crunchiness' but it had been replaced by a road surface infinitely worse. The lugs of lumber trucks had churned the track leaving horrendous corrugations. It was like driving through a furrowed field. One concise line in my diary reads: dreadful weather, dreadful cold, dreadful road. Because of the constant bumping it was impossible to write, but reading that, many years afterwards, sends a shiver through me.

"Is that a car crashed?" I heard myself warbling.

"Looks like one," Jeff answered softly, slowing down (well, going even slower than he was already). A telegraph pole was askew, its wires a tangle. When we drew level he stopped. The car, lopsided, was not completely covered by snow, suggesting that it had happened that day and the damage was not as extensive as might be expected following an encounter with the pole, but of the occupants not a trace. Where were they we wondered?

"Probably just ran out of road," Jeff said matter-of-factly, as if running out of road in the middle of an uninhabited winter wilderness the size of England was commonplace. I could hear Ben's warning ringing in my ears: "If you insist on driving through Northern Ontario 'to see Canada', you say, probably *all* you'll see will be the inside of a ditch."

But maybe Jeff was right not to be too alarmed, even though it was not exactly commuter country, the absence of the car's driver indicated that there was *somebody* else about if rescue were needed . . . Unless that somebody was a hungry bear!

A cluster of buildings in the distance heralded Hearst, a sawmill town in a French-speaking area, a mere sixty miles from Kapuskasing, yet it had taken us two and a half hours to get this far; already I was tense with tiredness (or tired because I was so tense?). While filling up with gas, Jeff noticed we had lost a wheel hub. "Should we go back to look for it!" he said. He bumped across the potholed road and drew up outside a building displaying a sign promising food; quickly mounting the steps we pushed open the door. A smell of stale cooking and tobacco wafted out. We closed the door again, remaining on the outside. It was snowing hard. We were thoroughly miserable. There was no other eating establishment that we could see. A case of Hobson's Choice: we went in; sat on tall stools at the counter and ordered coffee. With its drab, dark green painted walls and a single unshaded light, the place was gloomy like outdoors, but the piping hot coffee was reviving. Neither of us spoke. There wasn't anything cheerful to say. We knew the worst part of the journey lay immediately ahead and the weather was deteriorating rapidly.

The door was flung open. A couple of unshaven men, their faces weather-toughened, stood framed in the entrance. I almost expected them to whip out guns while shouting, "Your money or your life." Instead, they called out a friendly greeting, then clomped along the wooden floor, their huge, heavily mud-caked boots leaving a trail of miniature mud-castles behind them. Clumsily, they hoisted their bulky bodies on to stools beside us. It wasn't surprising the place didn't look smart if these were typical customers — in this part of the country lumber workers and miners would be the main clientèle. I watched the snow and mud slowly oozing from their garments mingling in dirty pools on the floor.

"Hiya!" one of them said, giving me a long look, before downing his coffee noisily in a couple of gulps. "It's not often we see women in these parts," he continued with a toothy grin. Unable to contain his inquisitiveness, "That your car with Tronna plates?" he enquired, inclining his head towards the door.

We nodded.

"No foolin'?" Black bushy eyebrows moved up his fore-head, his eyes widening in surprise, but he refrained from further questioning while he munched and supped. After a couple of minutes he was off again, "Howdya like that? From Tronna," he said, talking through his food, nudging his mate in the ribs with such force that the fellow's stool rocked on the uneven floor. Crumbs of bread dropping from his mouth, he asked us, "Where you headin' for?"

"Vancouver," we replied, as though it were the next town a few miles along a paved highway and here we were still in Ontario with the Prairies and Rockies yet to be negotiated.

"Vancouver!" he snorted, almost choking on his food. Then he fell silent.

Knocked him speechless, I thought laughing inwardly.

He recovered, "Y'mean Vancouver in British Columbia?" he quizzed, emphasising each word slowly, while poking the air with his fork held in his right hand.

"Yes, there isn't any other is there?"

"Nope, but *Vancouver*," he made it sound like another planet, "be 'bout three thousand miles away . . ."

"More," the other man interjected, speaking for the first time, without taking his eyes off his plate; he obviously wouldn't waste many words where one would suffice.

Then the inevitable question: "Whatja travellin' this way for?" the first man asked.

We attempted an explanation.

"Jes' but going *this* way to Vancouver . . ."

After a pause he said, "Your car's right well loaded."

Jeff answered the implied question, "We are moving house."

"Jes' movin' eh? Fancy that!"

Jeff asked him what the road was like out of Hearst.

With a long intake of breath he answered, "Bad at anytime of the year, but today, with the wet, pretty rough . . . you aint got lugged wheels or nothin' eh? . . . not easy in an ordinary car. Mightn't get through." His companion nodded in agreement.

I slid down from my stool. It was only then the truckers got a good look at me. On beholding my rotund figure they couldn't conceal their astonishment. The previously silent one said gravely – a whole sentence! – "Don't think *you* should risk it."

We thanked them and left. I could feel their eyes following us as we stepped outside into the swirling snow and imagined them saying, "Them guys are just plain nuts."

On getting into the car we discussed our predicament. If we continued we knew that we would have to travel two hundred and twenty-five miles (the distance from Southampton to Liverpool) to reach a hamlet with overnight accommodation and for *one hundred and thirty-five miles* of that, *there were no settlements* whatsoever along our route – no human contact, not even a non-human petrol pump – or we could traverse the road again to Kapuskasing. But then what? The roads were resurfaced with gravel from time to time, but when would that be? We even considered returning to Toronto, but we knew if we did, we could say good-bye to going to Vancouver. Jeff then suggested that I could travel part of the way by train and he would catch me up by car. When was there likely to be another train? We had seen one already that morning. Anyway, I considered travelling alone more frightening than to journey with him along dirt roads — at least that's what I thought at the time!

"I should never have come," he said dejectedly. "It is too much of a risk for you."

Although I, guilt-ridden, was thinking exactly the same, it had been a joint undertaking. Poor Jeff, I felt more sorry for him than myself. I tried to be cheerful. "Come on, if we don't get moving, the car will freeze to the road."

His arm around my shoulder, he pulled me towards him and kissed my hair. He slipped the car into gear. Less than a hundred yards further on we realised what the man meant by 'pretty rough' — the understatement of the year, or any year! Literally, the track was not rough, but soggy and full of holes, which gave the car a two-way motion as it bounced from hole to hole, while at the same time swaying sideways from rut to rut. Cartons and cases in the back rattled and creaked, but any concern about broken treasures was short-lived in our growing anxiety for ourselves. I was a bundle of nerves thinking what this shaking might do to me; I could well imagine what Jeff's fears were.

The wipers struggled to keep a crescent section of each window clear. Ice formed where it could. Occasionally, it became dislodged and slid in slow motion down the windscreen, obliterating our already restricted visibility. We passed a burnt out forest; the charred trees like blackened masts against the sky; death had passed this way casting its blight on all living things. Frequently we crossed racing rivers and swollen creeks, which had flooded their banks. We were on the map's single strand of road wending our way like a tortoise with a limp across hundreds of square miles of desolation.

After an interminable distance on straight road it must have been sod's law which determined that, when an enormous truck bore down on us (the first vehicle we had seen since leaving Hearst, two hours earlier) it was on an S-bend beside a gushing stream. Jeff pulled over quickly, our wheels actually in the murky water. The truck careered past, its giant, lugged wheels almost as high as our roof, the ground vibrating with the throb of its engine and the draught rocking the car, when it hurtled by. Splat. Splat. Our windscreen was sprayed with a gooey mixture of snow and red mud. The wipers worked overtime, but in vain. Jeff had to get out to scrape the window clear — well, clear of mud; the ice was too thickly encrusted to budge.

"It's bitterly cold," he said, hopping nimbly back in. "At least we are lucky the car is warm. Heavens!" he exclaimed looking at the mileometer, "Is that all we've done?"

It didn't seem possible, but the road got worse, thanks to that truck which had newly churned its surface. The car shuddered each time it hit a hole, then heaved as it lurched forward again, the wheels, like a treadmill gone haywire, spinning crazily on the slippery surface. The car made a sudden swerve and I burst into tears. Watching intently, Jeff tried to avoid the bigger pits, while I braced myself against the seat — no protective belts in those days. Zigzagging, with a top speed of fifteen miles per hour, his arms jerked now left, now right, his knuckles shining white through the flesh on his hands; gripping the wheel tightly, we ploughed through the ruts, sending tomato soup-coloured sprays of liquid mud into the air. Beads of perspiration glistened on his forehead making dark ringlets of his hair. He leaned close to the wheel peering through the ice-fringed window. What concentration, what skill he displayed. All I could do was to sit watching helplessly. We were traversing The Stretch.

Biting my lip to control sobs, hot tears ran down my face. For the first time in my life I wept with fear. The wipers whined as they flicked impatiently and there was the monotonous grind of tyres. The sounds echoing and re-echoing deceptively gathered momentum and volume. I struggled to be calm. I willed myself to breathe deeply, evenly. Dear God, would the car ever cease its jolting? I prayed. How I prayed, trying to subdue my mental turmoil. I wished I had listened to all those good people who had warned me of the possible consequences, if we travelled this way. Slowly, so very slowly, the miles crept up on the mileometer, while the car, like a tortured thing jerked its way forward foot by painful foot.

Jeff's voice broke the awful tension. He hadn't spoken for an age; driving claimed all his attention. "I think I can see paved road ahead." Then a minute or two later, "There is, there is," he said hoarsely. "There is!"

We reached it. The tyres touched solid ground.

"Whew!" he groaned, giving a long sigh. "Thank God," he said, pulling over to the side and stopping. "Thank God."

We sat in silence for a few minutes stunned by the ordeal. I was too overcome with relief to speak. It was like wakening from a nightmare to the glorious realisation that it was all over. Well, negotiating The Stretch was over. I hoped there wouldn't be any more road as bad. There couldn't be!

"There is some water in the flask," Jeff reminded me, rubbing his wrists vigorously. (We had forgotten to get coffee in it at the café.) "My arms will drop out of their sockets," he said wincing with pain, raising and lowering his shoulders, then stretching his arms in an effort to relax them. (For days afterwards he ached.)

It was more than three hours since we left Hearst and for that length of time he had been manoeuvring the car with no respite. I marvelled at his driving ability and endurance. Feeling gradually seeped back into my emotionally numb body. I sipped the cold water. Jeff drank thirstily.

"Better let the engine cool," he said scrambling out of the car. "It's red hot," he called, propping open the bonnet. He walked slowly around the car inspecting it. "A headlight has been smashed . . . and a hub cap . . . no, two hub caps are missing . . . mud . . . everywhere . . . it's covered, even the roof's caked with it . . . never guess it's blue."

I nodded absently in his direction. I hadn't yet spoken. I felt too drained.

"It's absolutely coated, like a hippo after a mud bath. Come and have a look. Come on."

"Come and have a look," I mimicked to myself. Typical of him. After what we had been through, now he was excited by the dirty appearance of the car! How quickly he adjusts . . . forgets what has gone before.

"Come on," he pleaded, laughing.

"No thanks," I croaked, finding my voice. "I believe you." I still felt as limp as a rag doll — quite exhausted with worry about the baby, apart from the fact that I ached all over. I was so relieved to be . . . to be? . . . yes, to be alive, that I was near to tears. How I admired him (though he wasn't the one who was pregnant!). He had nerves of steel. It would have been pointless to try to explain how I felt; I didn't try.

"A headlight smashed and two hub caps lost, that's all the damage I can see; but I hope water hasn't penetrated into the brake cylinders," he said, getting back into the car.

He looked so cheerful it was difficult to believe that he had just completed an extraordinary strenuous drive in a saloon car along a deeply rutted track in a blizzard! I leant my head against his shoulder. "What's the matter, feeling tired?" he asked. Oh Jeff!

The solitude was death-like; not a soothing tranquillity that enveloped the spirit, but rather an eerie stillness that plucked my taut nerves, underlining the loneliness and stark desolation of the vast surrounding country. Gradually the snow changed to rain. It began to wash the ice and snow from the windows. After half an hour, we felt sufficiently rested to resume our journey – or to be more accurate, I felt a *little* rested; Jeff had topped up the oil and then sat impatiently waiting for the engine to cool down.

(Long afterwards, when we were recalling this part of our journey, I asked him if he had been scared. He replied that, at the time keeping the car upright on the rutted track took all his concentration and, having negotiated it safely, there was no point in worrying about what might have been. For him, as always, the past was the past. What's the next challenge?)

"We'll stop in Longlac for a meal; I'm starving, are you?"

"Positively ravenous," I replied.

We passed a lumber camp situated on the far side of a huge expanse of bleak, dark lake water; the first sign of human life in three hours driving. How isolated it was. When you see the inhospitable surroundings in which the loggers work it is easy to understand their uproarious behaviour, whenever they hit town.

Longlac, with its promise of food, was not situated on the highway. We decided against turning off the good road, where we were able to travel relatively fast. We agreed to starve a bit longer. Late in the afternoon at a mining settlement, we stopped at a petrol station with an adjoining eatery. It was five hours since we had had coffee in Hearst and breakfast was three hours before that. After that length of time in captivity it was absolutely wonderful to walk again — so much for the doctor's advice about not sitting for long spells without some exercise! It was cold and miserable. We hurried through the rain to the snack bar; exercise would have to wait.

"Toronto plates," the girl commented, pouring our coffee.

During the next week I grew accustomed to being stared at in amazement when folk noted the Toronto car piled with our stuff and then took stock of me — *all* of me! While we were eating the rain dwindled and the clouds lifted. Weary of driving we were reluctant to resume our journey, but we had at least another hundred miles to cover before calling it a day. We wanted to get to a town where there would be a hospital in case . . .

The road out of Jellicoe was under construction and we had to follow a detour sign. It pointed through a wood. No! it wasn't an Irish joke; a bulldozer had cleared a path little more than a car's width through the trees. It was not a case of 'Here we go round the mulberry bush,' but straight on past the sumachs and birches bouncing over tree roots and dodging scrubby bushes, their branches brushing the car as we bumped along. I don't know what we were supposed to do if we encountered a vehicle coming the other way, because there wasn't room to pass, but luckily we didn't, and finally after a mile we were back on the highway. Later, these detour signs were a source of misery for us, but just then we were so elated at having cleared The Stretch, that a mere drive through a wood was but a pleasant interlude.

In the late afternoon the sun broke through the ragged clouds here and there, the patches of blue sky gradually increasing. The road continued west for a while and then dropped south. Simultaneously with the improvement in the weather the scenery changed dramatically. There were forests again for some miles and then a colourful, rugged landscape unfolded before us: stands of giant trees, startlingly blue lakes, rushing rivers topped with creamy foam and jutting everywhere rocks, a vivid red, all bathed in sunshine. What a transformation! What a contrast to that which had gone before. It was hard to believe just a few hours previously we had endured such misery. It had been an unfortunate combination of bad road and bad weather.

This was gemstone country: amethyst is mined in this western area of the province. Jeff was grateful for the good road surface and the fact that he could sit with his back supported by his seat instead of humped over the wheel trying to see the way. I was delightedly amazed by the improvement in the weather and temperature. Feasting my eyes on the magnificent scenery I nearly — but not quite! — forgot my nagging aches.

The town of Nipigon is situated on a river of the same name, where it flows into a bay on Lake Superior. The river drains Nipigon Lake: an enormous sheet of water set in a provincial park, but the highway didn't run near it. The town, famed as a tourist centre, looked prosperous in the evening light. Jeff drove into the carpark of an attractive hotel. "Like to stay here instead of a motel?" he asked. I readily agreed. Our room had a lovely wide view from its picture window. The clock, we noticed, was an hour earlier than our watches. We had crossed a time zone. We *were* making progress westwards despite all those difficult miles driving north!

Route 11 ended in Nipigon. The highway — a misnomer, surely, for the long stretches of gravel — had carried us *nine hundred miles* from Toronto through varied countryside, giving us a glimpse of how enormous and uninhabited Ontario was; until the approach road to the town, we could almost count the number of vehicles we had passed since leaving North Bay, two days earlier. To get to the province of Manitoba from Nipigon we would rejoin Route 17, many miles west from where it had fizzled out in Canada and merged with a Michigan State highway, to reappear again north of the forty-ninth parallel. It would be some years yet until the two sections of road met up to become the Trans-Canada Highway, Southern Route. The way we travelled, the only road then, is now called the Northern Route.

Before it grew too dark to see, Jeff attempted to clean the car, but all he succeeded in doing was to redistribute the mud. Not even Ben's team with their minute-car-wash technique would have had any more success. In a couple of hours, maybe, but certainly not in one minute!

## Chapter Ten

Shortly after eight we pulled out of the hotel carpark, resisting the temptation to stay for a few days' rest, or to explore the environs, the loveliest we had seen in Canada. The road, Route 17, skirted Lake Superior affording views of sunlit water. Another of the country's enormities, the lake covers an area the size of Ireland. There was some gravel road, bumpy in places. Jeff said we would have to stop in Port Arthur; water had seeped into the brake drums.

"They're not as good as they should be . . . will have to have them checked."

At least he admitted he was concerned, but it was months later before I knew why! In a throwaway remark one day he said, "Remember the drive from Nipigon to Port Arthur?"

"Yes," I agreed, expecting him to refer to the gravel road, the pleasant surroundings, maybe the warm sun, after the previous day's blizzard.

Instead, he said, "Did you realise we were travelling with very little braking?"

"Poor brakes?"

"Yes, for seventy miles."

"Oh Jeff!" was all I managed to say, when the horror of it, in retrospect, struck me speechless. My expressions of delight about the scenery had elicited nothing but grunts from him. No wonder!

Always glad of an excuse to get into oily overalls, he stayed at the garage, while I spent an hour having a look around. The twin cities of Port Arthur and Fort William, important ports, were then five miles apart. Port Arthur, on Lake Superior, a terraced city overlooking Thunder Bay, had a natural harbour for the ore and grain vessels plying the Great Lakes. On the waterfront I saw the gigantic grain elevators, some rising to two hundred feet. Over the years the city and neighbouring Fort William expanded and merged. In January 1970 they lost their old names to become Thunder Bay.

Fort William, the older of the two cities, was from early days a meeting place for native tribes and still had a large Indian population. The Hudson Bay Company had a fort here and traded in furs; beaver pelts, in particular, were sent to London, where they became gentlemen's top hats. There was a reconstructed fort, but we did not stop. We had lost precious time in Port Arthur; however, we allowed ourselves the luxury of a half-hour interlude at Kakabeka Falls. Often referred to as the Niagara of the North, they are situated on the Kaministikwia River, meaning the river with three mouths, steeped in local, Ojibway tribe, Indian lore.

At times like this we wished we were tourists and not hell bent on covering three thousand miles in as few days as possible. With camera and tripod we headed in the direction of the sound of water. Spray like fine rain made the ground marshy. Rustic bridges spanned small streams. Chipmunks and squirrels scurried from our path, not a human being in sight. We picked our way gingerly between tiny pools of iridescent water, glistening like giant soap bubbles. Then the falls came into sight: one hundred and twenty-eight feet of creamy foam cascading with an almighty roar into the tossing torrent below. It was possible to admire them at close range through a sturdy mesh fence. Surging billows of water soared high in the air catching the sunlight to shine in sudden brilliance for an instant before descending in a kaleidoscope of gorgeous colour.

"Come on, before you launch into lyrical ecstasies," Jeff teased. "We're getting drenched."

We moved back. While he was setting the camera on the tripod, a squirrel cheekily ran up to him, then sat watching quite unafraid, its tiny head cocked inquisitively to one side.

"Thinks your name is Disney," I said.

Tantalisingly tucked away among trees there was a motel,

but we daren't tarry. More gravel road and we lost another hub cap. That left only one. I wondered what bits of car might drop off next. Villages were sparse along our route and away from the highway there were few settlements. We were still very much alone. As always in Ontario, splashed in their hundreds were lakes like pieces of intricate lacework held together by blue ribbons of river. We had left behind the dense regimental forests of the north-east of the province for country that was only intermittently wooded. Trees fringed the grassy banks of rivers or grew in clumps on lake shores. Everywhere was green: the dewy green of spring.

I was feeling desperately tired but refrained from adding to Jeff's anxiety by admitting it because, despite his apparent easy-going attitude, I knew he worried constantly about me.

"Wonder what that is by the roadside ahead?"

It looked like a hoarding, but how incongruous in the middle of nowhere far from any town.

"It's a map," we exclaimed together when we drew level.

Jeff stopped. We climbed out of the car and crossed the road. A notice explained that Fort William had been a meeting place for native tribes; the accompanying map showed the route used by fur traders travelling between the interior and Fort William; the section of highway we had just covered ran directly over the old route. The years rolled away. I could picture Indians journeying through the bush transporting the valuable furs and skins of the animals they had hunted in the vast, unexplored-by-white-man hinterland and the rivalry between English and French traders. What a hard life it must have been! In the late twentieth century, with heightened awareness of *animal* rights, few want furs, but in the past they were a precious commodity. "The surroundings would be much as they are now," I thought — wild, lonely, dangerous, hauntingly beautiful. But what a different road! The completed part of the Trans-Canada Highway we were on stretched like a smooth, grey ribbon into the distance; at one point we noted that we could see six and a half miles ahead. The changing face of Canada: a new nation rising swiftly to replace the old.

We filled up with gas at a village called English River, wondering how it acquired its name. Now *there's* an undertaking for someone: to trace the origin of place names in Canada, or maybe something more manageable in one lifetime: in Ontario with its Indian, Inuit (Eskimo), European and British names.

"Not another detour," I groaned. A figure wearing a safety helmet stepped into the roadway waving a sign marked Slow in front of us before stepping back on to the verge. My smile of thanks froze, leaving me feeling like the Cheshire Cat, as I glanced at the expressionless face; not an eyelash fluttered; not a muscle twitched. He could have been a robot. Standing in the heat warning oncoming traffic was sufficiently exhausting I conceded guiltily without the added effort of being pleasant to grinning motorists. Sweat glistened on the bronzed torsos of the work crew, who all wore helmets.

While some gangs worked to tarmac lengths of gravel; others were busy repairing existing paving. As soon as the weather is favourable frost-damaged highways are made good, ready for the following winter's onslaught. Right across Canada we encountered roadworks. We became weary of being delayed, but what was worse were the numerous detours usually along potholed by-roads.

We stopped by a stream to finish our Toronto Coke and eat some fruit. The trees overhead, a froth of green lace, were alive with birds. Grasshoppers chirped. I lay back; shortly I was drifting towards delicious oblivion.

"Come on. I'm dead beat also. We can't afford the time to sleep," Jeff mocked, pulling me to my feet. Another short respite in Dryden for tea before tackling a further ninety miles, half of it on gravel surface. The clock on the dashboard ticked away relentlessly. I wriggled about trying to ease the dull ache that nagged down my back and legs. Jeff looked hot, dishevelled and exhausted. His ability to concentrate for hours on end as he did, without complaint, confirmed my long held opinion that I had married one great guy!

There were less trees now; the lakes multiplied. It was an incredible sight, looking more like a sea dotted with green islands than country broken by thousands of lakes, all shimmering golden in the late afternoon sun, but even a surfeit of beauty can pall in time, I thought gloomily. "Water,

water everywhere . . . " we were both parched and the water bottle was empty. The last fifty miles seemed intolerably long, but trees lining the road afforded precious shade. Their fresh greenness looked cool.

Four hundred miles and over eleven hours since setting out, decidedly frayed at the edges, we arrived, in Kenora, halfway across the continent of Canadian North America. Kenora, an important area for the Ojibway tribe of Indians, is situated on Lake-of-the-Woods, a popular resort, centre of a huge region famed for its hunting and fishing possibilities. It is reckoned that there are about fourteen thousand islands on the surrounding lakes with a shoreline of sixty thousand miles!

It was a humid evening without even the suggestion of a cooling breeze, when we set out for a ramble after dinner. The streets were dusty. Flies and mosquitoes swarmed. There were many Indians about, as there had been also in Port Arthur and Fort William, but our hopes of seeing any colourful characters were not realised; those we saw were unkempt, wearing ill-fitting western clothes in drab colours; some tired-looking; others disgruntled; many the worse for alcohol. A fracas developed between a wrinkled squaw, eyes black and shiny like onyx, and another with coal black hair and only a few teeth — the others lost in a previous encounter? We white skins deciding discretion being the better part of valour, retraced our steps to the hotel.

Our room was tastefully furnished, but stifling. Jeff sprawled in an armchair reading. I tried to concentrate on letter writing. A fan whirled ceaselessly, almost invisible in its speed, but to little effect; the air it stirred up was hot, and so moist it felt like liquid. Night fell. Taut with tiredness, sleep, for which I had longed all day, eluded me. I recalled the voices of office colleagues in Toronto.

"Kid, y'think our winters are miserable; wait til summer . . . it's unbearable with its damp heat. Honey you'll hate it. D'ya know we keep windows closed when the humidity gets real bad? . . . it's less hot that way. Yes, kid, it's cooler indoors, with fans working than out in the open . . . and then there's the mosquitoes!" I remember our first encounter with the double-glazed storm door at Ella's and how the perspex screens would have been replaced with mesh ones. Only the prosperous had air-conditioned cars and homes then, whereas today that comfort is commonplace. After days of hard driving we were still in Ontario, but I felt more determined than ever to reach the Pacific coast with its promise of a better climate.

A fly trapped behind the net curtains buzzed furiously jerking my mind back to the present. I opened the window wide. The insect flew off into the liquid darkness. I poked my head through the drapes. How right the girls were — it really was hotter outside! Jeff had been fast asleep for ages, tired out by the exertion of the day; he is not one to waste time tossing and turning with anxiety — ever. His thinking was: we had decided to go to Vancouver through Canada; that's what we were doing; we still had a long way to go; night-time was for sleep and recharging his batteries. Whether it was getting a job, when there were few available, or driving across a continent in an ancient car on poor roads, whatever the undertaking, his method was always the same: decide what had to be done. Consider the best way of doing it. Do it!

My legs were throbbing painfully; by the pale moonlight I could see my ankles were swollen. I dropped to the carpeted floor and rested my feet on the edge of the low settee. Sleep descended eventually.

"What are my feet doing up there? I've had an accident!" With a racing heart I sat up. At least I *am* able to sit up I thought with relief, looking about me. I climbed into bed. Sleep that 'blessed barrier between day and day' took over once more.

Next morning we got away early. Another day of cloudless skies was forecast, which would mean a repetition of yesterday's heat and glare. There was much to admire. Islands ablaze with flowering shurbs looking like enormous waterlilies floated on many lakes. The surface of others was almost entirely covered by log booms. In one devoid of logs two sea-planes like giant birds with silver wings were reflected in perfect detail in the water, part of the air ambulance service. The surrounding country consisted mainly of forest and there were few roads. Lumber crews were flown to their camps and in this land of lacustrine beauty that usually meant by sea-plane, float-plane they called it. Air transport plays an important role in the day-to-day life of Canada, among the world's first air-pioneered countries.

Water, the most prized of all nature's gifts, Canada has in abundance, one fifth of the world's fresh water — we had already seen much of it! Forests are another source of great wealth. The pulp and paper industry was one of Canada's biggest, yet each year fire, insects and disease consumed as much timber as the entire paper industry. We passed the first of many high lookout towers where a continuous watch is kept for the tell-tale blue haze in the distance: fire, the enemy which lurks ever-ready to feed its rapacious appetite.

Ahead a new road was being born. We had already had several detours but this time we had to stop because a truck had become bogged down. To the accompaniment of much gesticulating, a tank-like contraption manoeuvred its awkward bulk behind it and unceremoniously heaved it clear.

Good-bye Ontario! Just after nine o'clock we crossed the provincial boundary into Manitoba. It had taken us four days to travel through the province of Ontario, covering a distance roughly equivalent to that from Paris to Moscow. What varied scenery, what extremes of weather we had experienced; what fabulous wealth still lies beneath its surface; what a future it had, this Ontario to which we were bidding farewell; a farewell we hoped we would not regret.

One third of our journey had been completed. Highway 17 ended. From now on we would travel on Highway 1 across the provinces of Manitoba, Saskatchewan, Alberta and British Columbia to the Pacific coast. At last we were en route for Vancouver. Two thousand miles away? Yes! . . . but . . . all we had to do now was follow that road!

An avenue of trees, welcome for their shade, ended abruptly and we were in a large clearing. When our eyes adjusted to the sudden brightness we saw on our right the most exquisite lake we had yet seen: West Hawk Lake. A gem of such perfection it was stunning. Pines plunged their feet into the sandy foreshore; an island floated in the distance; to the west some dinghies were moored, the reflections of their red, warm yellow, and white hulls as sólid as the boats themselves.

On my eyes travelled to the heat haze on the horizon, back to the tree-fringed east shore. The whirr of the ciné camera, sounding staccato in the stillness, seemed an intrusion. Anyway, no picture could capture the magic of that moment. Beholding such beauty was a humbling experience.

We moved off slowly. Red petrol pumps stood out incongruously amid a group of pines on the far side of a wide clearing. A rustic, creeper-covered motel adjoined the small service station. Jeff pulled alongside for gas. Even if we had known about this lovely place the previous evening, it was unlikely that we would have driven this far, because it was nearing 7.30 pm when we reached Kenora, tired, thirsty and hungry.

The road surface was good. There was little traffic. For an hour or so we travelled along, not speaking much. I opened the map of Manitoba. It was not as vast a province as Ontario and how different it looked even on paper; gone were the masses of lakes, the network of rivers, the miles of road without a red dot denoting a village. Most of the lakes, enormous Lake Winnipeg and a scattering of others, were in the north of the province, but there were few marked along our route. There were rivers yes, but not in their thousands as in Ontario. The Trans-Canada Highway stretched in an almost straight line east west about sixty miles north of the American border, and was dotted with villages and towns. Roads, some paved, others gravel or dirt, reached to many parts of the province. Clearly we were not going to be isolated on this part of our trek.

Suddenly, we were on the Prairies! We were startled by the abruptness; there had been no gradual change of scenery. After our first sense of surprise had passed we were overawed by the vastness. As far as we could see in all directions the countryside rolled away. For days we had been driving through forests and had seen *billions* of trees! Now without their shade, the car soon became uncomfortably hot. The delayed after-effects of Monday's nightmarish drive would not be allayed: the familiar ache in my back was worsening. On we sped; the mileometer showed that, though the never-changing country beyond the car windows made it seem that we were not moving at all. Boredom permitted my mind full rein. Unanswerable questions chased one another like hobby horses getting nowhere. My self-accusations increased with each passing mile.

On the dual carriageway into Winnipeg, 'a metropolis in the middle of nowhere', the capital of Manitoba and the fourth largest city in Canada, it seemed strange driving in heavy traffic after days when long hours passed without *seeing* another car. We drove along Main Street until nearing the city centre before turning off to look for parking. Big, flashy cars with enormous tail fins, bumper to bumber, lined the kerbs.

"Give me the compact British car any day," Jeff said. "These stupid long cars take up so much space."

Realising that his temper was rather frayed, I declined to point out that we were driving a big car by British standards and the only reason it hadn't got tail fins was because it was an old model! A sign in a private parking lot warned, 'Unauthorised parkers will be towed away at their own expense'.

After nearly forty minutes we found a space.

We walked briskly along Portage Avenue, reputed to be one of the widest main streets in the world, but we were both more interested in food to assuage our considerable hunger — we had not had any mid-morning snack — than in admiring the architectural splendours of Winnipeg's shopping centre.

An hour later, after a satisfactory lunch in a Chinese restaurant, we were on our way again past shops and multi-storeyed offices, yellow and orange trolley buses clanging along the centre of the wide, straight street. There were some luxury apartment blocks and on the outskirts, attractive colour-washed bungalows set amid lawns with a profusion of flowers. I pictured these same bungalows in winter snow to the eaves for months on end. Winnipeg has been called the coldest place on earth! In January, when we were complaining about the weather in Toronto, a friend had had to visit Winnipeg. While there, he had been warned never to venture out, even momentarily, without warm protective clothing and to keep his mouth and nose covered at all times. He was introduced to The Winnipeg Shuffle: not a dance, but a way of walking using the minimum of effort to guard against breathing in too deeply and thereby freezing the lungs!

Pretty bungalows now — near-igloos in winter! What a country of extremes. The temperature was over eighty degrees Fahrenheit, yet two days previously in Northern Ontario it had been below thirty.

"Oh no, not along that!" I protested.

"Oh yes, unless you fit wings to the car," Jeff answered, when we encountered more road repairs and the detour sign indicated a corrugated track.

For the most part, though, the highway was a joy, which was just as well because there was nothing to see except prairie, passing through at speed was bad enough. Not even a nature poet is likely to burst into verse at the sight of the odd herd of cattle, while one occasional clump of bushes looks much like another. Four hours of sameness after leaving Winnipeg, we stopped in Brandon for gas. An advertisement in a window read: 'Custom Made Coats — Yaeger's Furs are from Trapper to You.' I silently hoped Jeff would suggest staying there for the night (not for the furs!); it was a good sized town with a choice of motels. Pigs (or cars) might fly! The garage clock indicated that we had crossed another time zone. Jeff remarked with delight that we had 'gained an hour' and we would 'forge ahead'. Forge ahead? At his words my heart plummeted: straight downwards into my sandals.

The clouds which had been scudding across the sky for some time went into a huddle, grew blacker, soon it was raining heavily. Drenched by the downpour the land stretched away dismally until its greyness merged with grey sky.

"We'll call it a day when we reach the next big town," Jeff said. "It's miserable driving in this."

I reached for the map, but a quick look showed, that apart from a few villages, with a population of less than a thousand, which were unlikely to have much in the way of overnight accommodation, there were no big towns for ages.

"There's one about thirty miles away: Virden. It should have a hotel." Alas, I failed to notice a small cross beside the dot on the map marking Virden, indicating it was an oil town. What an oversight!

Driving through I noticed that the crowds homeward bound were mostly men, and nearly all were tough-looking, bearded men. Strangely, I did not comment on it to Jeff, nor did he to me. We stopped outside the main hotel. Thoughts of a comfortable room, a relaxing bath, and appetising meal were beginning to dispel my overwhelming tiredness. But my rising spirits were dashed.

"The hotel's fully booked. Apparently there isn't another with vacancies nor are there any motels. Feel equal to travelling any further?"

"No, sorry darling, I just couldn't. Maybe there's a guest house, or something?"

A taxi driver was standing outside the hotel. Sure, he knew a place . . . "Nothin' ver' swell y'know . . ." but if we would hang on for a few minutes he would be taking a passenger to that address.

Shortly, without looking in our direction, accompanied by a bearded man, the driver jumped into the taxi and took off at a speed capable of sending him into space, roaring along narrow streets like a demented thing, careering crazily round corners, only to accelerate even more when he levelled out. The fact that the road surface was potholed deterred him not at all. Frightened at losing sight of him, we followed in a fog of fumes and dust, which did little for my frayed nerves.

Four or five seemingly interminable minutes later, without any signalling, the taxi jerked to an abrupt halt. Jeff had to slam his brakes hard to avoid ramming him. We had arrived! There was no sign of the house; it was hidden from view by bushes.

"Here we are," the driver beamed triumphantly — as well he might: it was a miracle we were still alive. "You guys'll get fixed up, that's for sure," and he took off again like a bat from hell.

His passenger, a shifty-looking character, was already making his way in the direction of the house; we followed through the gateless entrance in the house-hiding hedge. A path of cracked paving, barely discernible through a conglomerate of weeds, led to a rambling structure, its woodwork shedding tears of dingy, dark brown paint; the front porch with sagging roof looked about to part company with the rest of the building. Several lean-tos propped here and there suggesting that, whenever the need for extra space had arisen, they had been constructed at random without any regard for architectural appearance. It was now a case of what was supporting what, because the whole place looked on the verge of collapse.

Our new-found friend was already ringing the bell, which clanged discordantly. Broken glass; dried-out garden pots filmy with cobwebs; discarded furniture littered the porch. The whole house appeared to have given up living decades ago. It would have made a good set for a horror movie. By this time we were prepared for anything. The door was opened, surprisingly not by a weird character, but by a middle-aged, pleasant-looking woman.

"Come on in," she said encouragingly in a western accent, stepping to one side. She obviously was expecting our companion and directed him to his room before speaking to us. Amazement registered on her face on taking stock of me, but she made no comment. We asked if she had a room vacant.

"Well folks, you're in luck."

We all climbed up a narrow staircase to a dark landing, off which there were three doors, painted with the same brown paint as the exterior of the house. Whatever kind of luck she was referring to it wasn't the good variety. She opened one of the doors. I took a cautious step inside. What a room! It was unbelievable! There were two iron bedsteads; three chests-of-drawers liberally layered in dust; a mirror so dirty it gave back no reflection; a long-dead aspidistra in a cracked pot stood atop a pile of yellowing newspapers; and empty condensed-milk tins decorated the furniture like objects d'art.

"Heavens! No!" I almost blurted out, then extreme tiredness prompted me to check the bed coverings. They were clean. We decided to stay. On request I was then escorted to the bathroom. An escort was necessary. The bathroom was downstairs. Leading off each other there was a succession of rooms crammed with furniture. A sitting-room — one of many — was traversed turning right at a piano, then left past a cluttered table, through a connecting door to a dining-room, skirting several more tables, across the kitchen, then down a dark passage . . . And we were there. It felt as if we had walked back to Winnipeg. The bathroom was small with irregular walls and a sloping tin roof. It must have been one of the many haphazard additions we had seen from outside. Unexpectedly, there was a porcelain wash-basin. Grubby? Yes. Cracked? Yes, but the water was warm. A spider crawled around the plug hole. I had a wash, combed my hair, set my compass and rejoined Jeff in the hall.

"Thought you'd got lost," he said, taking my arm, steering me out into the welcome fresh air.

We had not the foggiest idea where we were, except that it was a distance from the main street. I felt so wretched I had no inclination for food at all, but Jeff, understandably, was starving.

In a café my pregnancy and Jeff's clean-shavenness made us conspicuous because the customers were all hairy males. The food was much better than the surroundings had augured. Afterwards, following conflicting directions, we wandered looking for a church — the following day was Ascension Day and we hoped to get Mass before leaving town. Finally, we were thoroughly lost! Jeff usually has a good sense of direction, thus by now he was decidedly cranky.

"I can't walk any further," I said; for some time my feet had been moving independently of the rest of my body. "There's nobody about; I'll sit on the edge of the pavement here, while you scout around."

I hoped I wouldn't be mistaken for a drunk, but, utterly jaded, I didn't care. The sound of rustling leaves in a bush behind me penetrated my numbness. I looked in the direction of the noise and saw the face of a small child peering inquisitively through the branches. There were squeals of delight. I was too tired to respond. Derisive laughter erupted: two small children were standing near me on the gravel sidewalk. I managed a wan smile. One, then the other, stuck out a tongue in reply. Nobody spoke. I smiled again. Out popped the tongues accompanied by giggles at their bravery. "Better get to my feet." Adults would come searching for the tongue-pullers before long.

The bedroom, when we returned was like a bake-house, the sun streaming through the closed sash window. After a struggle, Jeff got it open but the cords were broken. By standing several of the empty condensed-milk tins one on top of another he propped it open a couple of feet. I felt exhausted to the point of illness. Jeff suggested calling a doctor. I declined. The thin curtains shut out some of the light; despite the brightness (it was nine o'clock), the narrowness of the bed, and the decidedly lumpy mattress, I quickly fell asleep.

I could hear voices . . . loud voices . . . men's voices. My heart was thundering.

"Where didja get that shirt?"

"Whose jacket's that?"

The mumbled replies were inaudible.

"Are you awake?" I heard Jeff whisper from his bed on the far side of the room. So it wasn't a dream.

"Well, where didja get 'em?" came the sharp demand.

Another slurred reply. The voices were in the next bedroom, the one occupied by our taxi-passenger friend.

"Come on with us."

There was much shuffling on the landing outside our door followed by thump, thump, thump down the stairs.

"What time is it?"

Jeff looked at the travel alarm clock, "One o'clock."

The fumbling footsteps were now in the porch below us.

"Come and look . . . quick . . . " Jeff said at the window.

Barefooted, I crossed the dusty linoleum to see our friend being led away, between two officers of The Mounties: The Royal Canadian Mounted Police.

## Chapter Eleven

"He said he was looking for the bathroom."

"The bathroom!" I echoed.

On the way back from my ablutions before seven, the lady-of-the-house waylaid me apologising for the night-time disturbance."

"We heard him banging about . . . found him rummaging in the wardrobe. He was wearing some of my husband's clothes . . . even a tie . . . over his pyjamas. He said he was looking for the bathroom. He was drunk," she added, unnecessarily, I thought.

Poor bloke, the bathroom was difficult to locate when sober . . .

"I was sure worried about *you*. Guess you felt mighty frightened?"

It transpired that we had only surfaced from unconsciousness towards the end of the episode. The flashy dresser was a 'wanted' man.

After the departure of the Mounties we had had a long wait until the house fell quiet, then I coaxed Jeff to accompany me to the aforesaid bathroom, because I was too scared to attempt the journey alone, yet at that time, we were ignorant of the fact that the inaccessibility of the place had played a part in the night-time visit of the RCMP!

"See you're from Ontario. Goin' on vacation?"

Our muddy Dodge, rear end close to the road, the interior piled with heterogeneous junk, staying overnight in a dump like this . . . some vacation!

"We are moving to Vancouver," I explained.

"You don't say," she said, eyes widening, eyebrows

disappearing under her fringe. "Goin' south to the States? Where're you crossin'?" The orbs and arcs returned to their normal position.

"We're not, we're driving through Canada."

"Through the *Rockies?*" Her voice went up this time.

"Yes."

"You don't say."

I felt awkward standing there in my dressing-gown, towel and sponge bag in hand, while she surveyed me. She smiled apologetically. I wasn't sure whether she was regretting her previous inquisitiveness, or was apologising in advance for her continued curiosity, because she promptly started to question me at length. Why were we moving to Vancouver? When was the baby expected? Had I made arrangements with a hospital? What were our prospects of getting jobs? Accommodation? . . . All the niggling worries that had beset me, whenever I allowed my mind to wander unchecked, she put into words, dousing my spirits. I am sure she meant well. She seemed kind; concerned on our behalf. In fact, her very appearance: plump, apple-cheeked, middle-aged, with a pleasant voice, in full possession, it appeared, of all her faculties, physical and mental, standing amid the grubby clutter made me want to fire questions at *her.* How *could* she live in a place like this, let alone charge people to stay there? What about our room? Apart from changing the beds it hadn't been cleaned for aeons. Most strange of all the peculiarities, outdoors and inside, were the dozens of empty condensed-milk tins. Did each bedroom have some? Did she know there was a calendar on the back of the bathroom door open at August last year. Had nobody been in there since then?

Instead, I murmured that it was time we were on our way and retreated upstairs to get ready.

"Gee I won't forget this place in a hurry," Jeff said, as he stowed the case in the boot of the car.

It was a sultry morning, raining slightly. In a matter of minutes we reached the church. If only we had gone by car the previous evening . . . There was only a handful at early Mass, mostly women – there *were* women in Virden! Afterwards we had a quick breakfast and back to the car, where

Jeff put his foot down hard on the accelerator and we sped along the road and out of town.

Half an hour later, a flight of wild ducks flew low in front of us heading north, when we drove into Saskatchewan: province number three. On making a rough calculation, we realised that we were more than halfway between Toronto and Vancouver. "The going for the next couple of days on the prairie highway should be good," Jeff said.

We would make it to Vancouver. We *would*. Where there's a will . . .

The clouds were lifting. There was little of interest to see. A few brown cows grazed peacefully and here and there, dotted on the flat countryside, machines, so far away they looked like busy mice, scuttled backwards and forwards sowing grain. The highway was excellent and we travelled along effortlessly.

We overtook a home-on-wheels being towed behind a big, shiny Oldsmobile; it was quite a large house, colour-washed pale pink. I was blasé about such sights now, but I'll always remember the first occasion I saw a house being transported in that way. It was outside Toronto. We were in Ben's car. Feeling pretty sick, I was sitting silently in a corner back seat gazing through the window. Heavens! I would have to ask Ben to stop . . . my dizziness was worsening . . . the very houses were moving before my eyes: *there* was one travelling along – a big, mauve bungalow with white paintwork. My heartbeats quickened . . . it was coming nearer. Eva's calm voice arrested my mounting panic, "Look at that house being towed."

Much employment in Canada was seasonal or contractual. Sometimes, employees might have been lucky to stay in one place for a couple of years; other times only for a few months. Accommodation in out-of-the-way locations is difficult to obtain; often family men invest in a transportable house. They are lovely with living-room, bedrooms, kitchen, laundry-room, the works . . . When it is time to move, the house, with all its contents, is jacked up then lowered onto a special frame with bogie wheels – the family is mobile again. Their next destination reached, the house is positioned on prepared foundations. A garden is cultivated and within a matter of weeks the place has the appearance of permanency.

Moving houses was nothing new in Canada; originally it was done by horse and buggy.

(Some fifteen years after we left Toronto, a very famous house was relocated. Historic Campbell House, one of the earliest and largest brick residences built in York [Toronto's name at the time] for Scottish-born Sir William Campbell, in the first years of the nineteenth century, was moved to a new site. To facilitate this it was necessary to clear electricity and telephone poles, traffic lights and signs, eighty-two street lamps and nearly a mile of trolley wire [no street-cars running that day!]. Sixty-five manhole covers on the route had to be reinforced. It took six hours to make the one mile journey. The next day, when the house was lowered onto its new foundations it was only a half-inch out of line with the survey!)

Overhead became a dome of deep blue. The temperature was eighty degrees and climbing. Wheat fields shimmering golden stretched endlessly into the heat-haze. The road, a peculiar yellowish shade: reflected colour from the grain, like a taut ribbon, unwound into infinity. We were glad of our sunglasses. We passed through small towns, slowing down to the authorised thirty miles per hour. Each town looked an exact replica of the last; there was little to distinguish it from any other prairie village. Each had its giant granary of prosaic, angular outline, one or two spired churches, homesteads and small stores clustered together. We would pass through in a matter of minutes; then the road (so straight we could see ahead for seven miles) into nowhere until thirty or forty miles further on we reached the next village.

How desolate they must be in winter. No protection from harsh, Arctic winds, blinding blizzards, drifting snows — it's not surprising the houses gather together in the shelter of their granary; and in summer no protection from the scorching heat, the smothering dust. Temperatures range from fifty below zero to one hundred degrees Fahrenheit. The prairies breed a tough people, they have to be, their very survival depends on it.

Mile after mile, hour after hour we drove on through

wheatlands, no trees, no hedgerows, no rivers, no lakes, nothing but golden flatness: 'Fields of grain that stretch from sky to sky'. The telegraph poles marched in an unbroken line, distance diminishing them to matchsticks. The sun blazed down relentlessly and the heat was thrown back from the ground to hang in the breathless air.

The villages had lovely names, Elkhorn, Moosomin, Red Jacket, Summerberry. We pulled up at the roadside near Sintaluta for a picnic. We got out. Whew! The heat rose in blistering billows. With no shelter from the searing sun we decided to eat in the car. There was a rail-track nearby. A freight train passed. We lost count after seventy-eight wagons, our eyes following it, the only moving object, until the black speck disappeared in the void. There had been no settlers in this part of Canada before the coming of the train, towards the end of the last century. Having eaten and quenched our thirst with water – a horrid lukewarm liquid – we were on our way again, why dally in this heat?

A service station was being built by the side of the highway. We passed a tall beacon with a notice Speed Laws Enforced by Radar; the excellent road abetted fast driving. There were more villages with intriguing names, Indian Head, Qu'Appelle, then in the distance we could see smoke from oil wells at Pilot Butte. Presently a forest of erect TV aerials heralded the approach to Regina (named after Queen Victoria). Jeff slackened speed. Oil refineries, gas stations, motels and drive-in cinemas flanked the highway on both sides into the capital of Saskatchewan; it looked like any mid-west town we had seen in American movies. That old enemy, time, decreed that we should not delay. We drove straight through Regina, down wide, tree-lined Victoria Avenue – another line of trees down its centre – turned into Albert Street skirting Wascana Park, crossed the bridge over Wascana Lake and on past Government Buildings in their landscaped grounds. After passing many hundreds of thousands of lakes in the early days of our trip, we were amused to learn that Wascana was an *artificial* one. It had been created by damming a creek called Pile of Bones. It was only six feet deep.

The headquarters of one of the world's largest grain-handling organisations and also the Royal Canadian Mounted Police were in Regina; but despite the importance of the city, the lovely homes, wide streets, everywhere clean and bright, impressive public buildings, the valiant effort to create a languid lake it seemed to be, not a city, but an overgrown prairie village, surrounded as it was by open fields.

The highway out was under repair. We bumped along unceremoniously for a few hundred yards and then were back on good road again. A haze had smothered the sun and was creeping over the flat countryside. The temperature was ninety-five. Occasionally, a gust of hot wind struck the car rocking it teasingly before dying away only to return each time with greater force. It blew sand across the road.

With a sudden s.w.o.o.s.h the capricious wind dislodged something from the back of the car. It passed at terrific speed between our heads and through the open window on my side to disappear immediately from sight. Jeff stopped.

"What was that?" he asked amazed.

"I don't know. It went so quickly, I didn't see it."

I knelt on the seat and leant into the back of the car, mentally checking the contents of the various cartons and boxes.

"Oh it must have been the one with my hats," I wailed. My two precious wedding hats!

We stood by the roadside looking about us. Not a sign of them. There were no ditches or hedges where the truant carton could be lurking.

"How extraordinary," I said.

Together we crossed the highway to search the other side. I blinked several times thinking my eyes were to blame for the distortion. Jeff's voice jolted me to action.

"A storm! Back to the car. Quick! Quick!"

The wind almost sweeping us off our feet as we ran, hats forgotten, Jeff dragging me frantically behind him, we groped for the doors, tumbled in and closed all the windows. Despite the heavy load, the car began to sway with the buffeting.

"Good God that wind is strong," Jeff said, an anxious edge to his voice.

"We are very exposed here . . . " I gasped — the dash

along the highway had left me breathless.

"Maybe it would be better if we were moving," he shouted above the noise of the wind, releasing the handbrake and driving off quickly.

It grew steadily hazier. The vast prairieland was shrouded in a blanket of dust, which swirled and eddied, greatly restricting visibility. The wind gave us wings. The car felt airborne, as we streaked along, Jeff humped over the steering-wheel, eyes probing the grey fog, which completely surrounded us. It was difficult to see the road, but whenever he slackened speed the car began to shake. It happened with such swiftness there was no time to be frightened. The wind roared deafeningly and with turbulence; I half expected at any moment we would be sucked high into the air like the house in the Wizard of Oz.

Thirty minutes later the wind died as suddenly as it had risen. Thank God it had only been a brief storm. Breathing deeply with relief Jeff pulled on to the hard shoulder.

"Have we any water? Lukewarm or not it will do," he said, mopping his sweaty brow. "Hope we don't have any more of those . . . " he went on, between gulps. His driving skills daily were being tested. "Wonder what happened to your hats . . . want to go back?" he joked.

A surprise for someone; one exclusive hat had a London label, the other a Dublin one. Not much good for the prairie sun, though!

Dust hung like fog. It would take hours for it to settle. Moose Jaw was enveloped in a haze when we stopped for ice-cold milk shakes, which did little to clear our throats. Perched on an incline we should have had a panoramic view but there was nothing to see but gloom. The car was thickly coated. Jeff washed over the windows; I brushed what dust I could off the front seat.

"It's got chilly," I said shivering.

On the car radio we heard that winds were still gusting at sixty miles an hour and the temperature had dropped twenty degrees in two hours. Chilly? It was now seventy-three degrees – a hot summer's day, back home! Jeff had to swerve to avoid a family of ducks, which waddled leisurely across the highway in the direction of a pond, the surface of which was blurred by the breeze. We passed what looked like sand-dunes; it was a golf course. The countryside became undulating and the dust in the air lessened. In the distance sheep and lambs dotted the pale green hillocks. The road continued straight for miles. Time passed tediously. Jeff was happier when driving required concentration and skill; rolling along at a steady pace for hours on end he found boring.

At Swift Current we filled up with petrol. Oil had been discovered in this area and there were hopes that beneath its prairies Saskatchewan would uncover wealth equal to that already found in the oil-fields of the neighbouring province of Alberta. (We know those hopes were fully realised.) The garage attendant wore a big hat, a checked shirt with a neckerchief and spoke with a twangy western drawl. Cowboy country, I thought, with childlike delight. Because, in Jeff's words, we had gained another precious hour, we pushed on a further forty miles to Gull Lake.

Set well back from the road, in the middle of nowhere, the motel window gave us an uninterrupted view of the rolling prairies. My weariness slipped away like a discarded coat. Our drive — three hundred and eighty miles — in exchange for views like this was worthwhile.

"Have a look," Jeff called when he opened the boot to get our bag. What a mess! There was a mound of fine grey dust. For weeks afterwards we were shaking it out of things.

We had showers before eating at the adjoining café. Later, I resisted the urge to sink into an armchair; instead I sat at the writing desk in this beautifully appointed room — what a contrast to our last one! — to write to my parents. I scored through the name of the motel and wrote underneath c/o Hasting Street Post Office, Vancouver; I explained that we had no forwarding address. Should I describe in graphic detail all that had happened or just enumerate the pleasant aspects? I decided on the latter. It was kinder. At the end I wrote, 'Will write when we reach Vancouver.' I remained sitting lost in thought: we had yet to negotiate the Rockies...

Jeff got to his feet, breaking off my day-dreaming. "It's too dark to read," he said, crossing the room.

"I'm stiff," I complained, joining him at the window.

"Poor darling," he said softly against my hair, putting

an arm around me.

We stood gazing out. Nothing stirred in the enormous world outside. Our own breathing was the only sound. The warmth had gone out of the sky and the sun, a crimson ball, shed its rays across the flat, hushed land. Slowly it slipped, singeing some fleecy clouds with fire and brightening the deep evening sky with streaks of light. Enthralled, we watched the fingers of flame across the earth grow paler to vanish swiftly, wiped away by an unseen hand. The glow faded from the clouds. Darkness crept stealthily across the sky, then as the sun dropped towards the horizon, a half-moon shone silver in the purple heavens. Moon and sun together, night determinedly taking over before dilatory day had bade a reluctant farewell. The red horizon turned to pearly pink then gradually dimmed. The giant curtain of night descended. The sun slid out of sight. Day had ended. Night now reigned supreme.

Refreshed, and in good spirits, we were on our way again early next morning. Another beautiful day. Another excellent road, straight and well-paved, which we had grown to expect on the Prairies. The homesteads at first scattered sparsely near the town became non-existent. Trucks full of workers shunted on the nearby rail-track.

"Look, there's a cowboy."

"A cowboy! Where?"

"Over there." Jeff pointed to the left.

"Oh stop, please."

Astride a magnificent, black horse, complete with spurs and wide brimmed hat the cowboy gracefully manoeuvred, rounding up cattle, which trotted ahead of him like sheep before a collie, tiny calves darting in and out of the herd anxiously seeking their mothers. Shading my eyes with my hand, I watched them move away into the distance. I, who dislike Western films, my scathing remarks about celluloid cowboys meant my loathing was no secret, was all aquiver at having seen my first cowboy in the flesh. Passing motorists, too, also wore the customary head gear: ten gallon hats.

Jeff teased me unmercifully: "Never again claim boredom at a Western."

We left Saskatchewan. Just after nine we were into Alberta, rolling cattle country, and three quarters of an hour later we arrived in Medicine Hat, passing through more small towns with granaries along the way. In the previous three days we had crossed provincial borders early in the morning. Though we had not planned it that way, it meant we stayed in a different province each night.

Medicine Hat proved to be an attractive place, bristling with vitality, with an absence of overhead wires, which spoil the skyline of many Canadian towns. With limitless amounts of natural gas available, at one time it was considered less costly to keep the gas street lights burning all the time, than to extinguish them during daylight. Fascinated by the name, I solicited an explanation, none was convincing; and despite later searching books for an answer, its origin remains obscure. We bought food for our lunch, fruit and a carton of drinks before leaving.

The open prairies of Manitoba had given way to vast wheatlands in Saskatchewan, which in turn was succeeded by rich, ranching country in Alberta; always the highway cut through: a smooth, wide swath over one thousand miles of almost straight road with few twists or turns. Can you imagine it? In multi-countried Europe is there a long, unbending road anywhere?

A grey hare darted across the highway in front of us. Plump, black birds with shiny coats and red wings flitted about. Once in a while, crows wheeled or swooped. Deer ambled, suggesting that wooded country was not far off. The odd flock of sheep; lots of brown, rough-coated cattle grazing, but no more cowboys in action. Apart from an occasional car, there was little sign of human life. Jeff looked more relaxed and cheerful than he had done for days, even though he preferred more challenging driving. In a little over three hours we covered two hundred miles.

At noon we stopped to have a picnic. While I was tidying up afterwards, Jeff decided to have a look at the engine. If I had had my wits about me, tactfully, I would have suggested waiting till later, but somehow it didn't seem necessary, because he said it would only take a couple of minutes. Forty minutes later, I asked if he was going to be much longer.

"Just coming," he called in a muffled voice.

Another five minutes passed before he emerged from under the bonnet. What a sight!

"I'll be with you in a moment," he said with a childlike grin, obviously oblivious to the length of time he had been tinkering with the engine, to say nothing of the mess he looked.

"What was the matter?" I enquired when he got back into the car.

"Nothing," he replied a little sharply, implying that I had a nerve to even suspect that something could be wrong with the engine of *his* car!

"Wonder where I'll get some water for a wash?" he asked.

"I wonder," I said, sarcastically, gazing about me at the waterless countryside.

"Guess I'll have to wait until we book into a motel."

"Guess you will."

(The car was a recent acquisition, so I did not realise yet how much loving care he would lavish on this and all subsequent vehicles, and not just his own either. He was a genuine car physician, an excellent mechanic. Ben had once said jokingly that Jeff could tell what was wrong with a car by its colour! If a vehicle needed attention it got it regardless of whether or not he was attired for dirty work. I recalled his mother telling me once, that she had known Jeff to do a job on an engine while he was wearing evening dress!)

About fifteen miles east of Calgary we saw them; got our first glimpse of them far away on the horizon. We wondered if it might be cumulus, but looking more intently we could discern their jagged peaks thrown into prominence against the sky, when the sun struck their snowy upper regions. The Rockies. The Rockies at last! Later that day, we discovered that we had first seen them from sixty miles away.

We drove into Calgary at two-thirty, City of the Foothills, three thousand, four hundred and thirty nine feet above sea level, known as the Sunshine City, because it has more than two thousand hours of sunshine annually, not necessarily hot sun, much of it is during winter. The locality can have snow, frost or hail in any month of the year. Each July they have their famous stampede, with broncos, steers, wild cow milking, calf-roping and careering chuck-wagon races. At one time called Cow Town, it was now an industrial centre and shipping port for the oil-fields. It would have been nice to have a look around; but we drove straight through, passing small shops advertising cowboy boots and clothing, and were back on the highway by two-fifty, which gives an indication of how compact the city was then, with few of the skyscrapers which dominate it today.

The road became winding with a gentle climb through countryside, which was very green. There were trees again. About two and a half hours after first sighting the Rockies we entered **Banff National Park**, roughly the size of Devon, in the beautiful Bow Valley at an altitude of over four thousand feet. It was six months since we had admired the photograph of Banff on a menu card on board the *Empress of Britain* — little knowing then that we would visit it. And so soon! This we hoped would be the highlight of our transcontinental journey. After a week driving through flat country, following six months living in flat Southern Ontario, the mountains crowding us made us shrink with claustrophobia. Looking out the side window I had to strain my neck to see the snowy summits.

Banff, a famous ski resort, had visitors all the year round, though some of the hotels, including The Banff Springs, were only open for part of the year. The summer season commenced on June first, which was the following day; it was also Jeff's birthday.

"Timed it nicely," he said, "this is the last day for off-peak rates."

There were plenty of motels all smart and attractive, some brightly painted lined up in regular formation; others, their timber walls polished to a high gloss, sprawled haphazardly beneath giant fir trees, which dwarfed them to playhouses. We booked a rustic unit. A split-door, hinged like a stable door, gave access to the main room. Off it was the shower. Most of the furniture was pine with the divans, chairs and windows draped in chintz. Not surprisingly, there pervaded everywhere, both indoors and out, the spicey aroma of pine. I was terribly excited. Those long days on the road had not been in vain.

"Suppose I need a shower?"

I looked at his oil-streaked face, his tousled hair clinging in damp curls to his sweaty forehead, his grimy hands, crumpled shirt and answered in one word, "Yes!"

Presently, we set out walking into town. It was an attractive place, uncommercialised, with no gaudy advertisements, or neon signs. Shop windows displayed quality wares — Irish linen, Waterford cut-glass, Beleek china, English bone china, Scottish tweeds and tartans, cameras and photographic equipment, silverware, French perfume — all of foreign origin; lovely Indian leather craft and beadwork were, sadly, the only Canadian items to be seen. (Today, there is plenty to choose from in the way of Inuit [Eskimo] and First Nation [Indian], in addition to more recent natives' work, on sale in attractive stores, or to be seen in museums, across the continent.)

After a leisurely dinner we set off down Banff Avenue, over the bridge spanning the Bow River to ramble on in contented silence for some time through the pines and evergreens along its banks, disturbing grazing deer, which trotted off into the wilderness. To the east, backed by Sulphur Mountain, lay Banff Springs Hotel with its outdoor swimming pools, where one can swim in the waters of natural sulphur springs. There are several pools with temperatures ranging from seventy-eight to one hundred and twelve degrees Fahrenheit. It was a pleasure I had to forgo, although Jeff did not feel deprived; he hates swimming and watersports. We walked back, pausing on the bridge. It afforded a wonderful vista. In front of us there was Banff Avenue, the main street, which appeared to run slap bang into a pointed mountain. Midas-like, the mellow sunlight turned everything to gold. Clouds, which hung low over the distant ranges, caught fire in the setting sun to blaze for a while in bright orange, before gradually fading. It became cooler.

We approached our motel. Slung low between tree trunks, looking incongruous in these surroundings, more like a European campsite, there were clothes lines. I, too, did some washing and hung it out on a piece of rope, tied between the doorpost and a nearby tree — one night free from the ping pong of water dripping in the shower. By the time I had finished daylight had gone. Jeff silhouetted against the window was all I could make out in the darkness, when I returned indoors.

"Come and see the view."

I crossed to his side. The mountains looked enormous in the night. A myriad of stars studded the navy blue sky. There was no movement except a ruffling in the treetops when the slight breeze sifted through them. Banff at night: another magical memory for my storehouse.

## Chapter Twelve

A shaft of light penetrating between folds in the curtains and falling diagonally across the room, woke me early. I, who normally find it difficult to come to life in the mornings, who have a reputation for being unapproachable before nine, quickly bounded out of bed full of enthusiasm for the day ahead. I opened the top half of the door. The air smelled delicious. Dew sparkled in the trees and carpeted the grass. Some deer were grazing on the open space nearby.

"What time is it?" sleepily grunted Jeff, who probably thought it was mid-morning because I was dressed.

"Just after six-thirty," and not giving him a chance to voice amazement — or concern! — at my high spirits at this hour, I added, "Many happy returns. Come on Methuselah; it's too good a day to waste in bed. I've been up for ages." It was his twenty-fifth birthday.

Not having to vacate the motel until noon, we decided to have another look at the town before leaving. After breakfast in a coffee shop, we strolled through the rock gardens, built in a series of rock plateaux with an abundance of alpine plants and tiny waterfalls tumbling from pool to pool. We visited the government museum. Show cases had natural history exhibits: enormous grizzly bears; giant moose and elk; specimens of fish; various birds including a golden eagle; butterflies in a marvellous array of colours; insects and flies — all had been caught, trapped or slain in the neighbourhood of Banff. There was also a fascinating collection of native Indian relics and handiwork: tepees, wigwams, canoes, tomahawks; displays of garments encrusted with beautiful beadwork; feathered head-dresses; and — hideous to look at – shrunken, scalped skulls. All these were now precious museum pieces of great interest, but how short a time ago, a little over one hundred years, since Indians, alone, inhabited this magnificent, wild country and the white man was almost unknown in Western Canada. What a young country it is! Some of the early maps had huge tracts of land left blank because they were unexplored, these were encased in glass to preserve them. There were paintings and yellowed photographs of the explorers and founders of the new Canada. We could have browsed for days, but our old enemy was barking at our heels. Outside, our eyes were blinded by the glare after the restful shade indoors.

We sent cards to our parents to prove we had got this far safely, then back to the motel; packed the cases in the boot; took a last admiring look about us and were on our way. There was a gravel surface, dry and level, on this part of the Trans-Canada Highway, Route 1, heading for Lake Louise.

Cutting through a forest, the narrow road was lined on both sides by tall conifers, which went on and on until the parallels seemed to converge in the far distance. We passed a by-road leading to Mount Norquay, which featured the Banff chairlift, the only chairlift at the time in the Rockies; famous because it was one of the highest and longest in the world.

"Can you imagine what the view must be like from the top? . . . would love to come here in winter . . . I might even get to like snow," I said.

"Huh!" Jeff replied. "Get to like *snow?* In that case we might as well have stayed in Toronto," he retorted, not unreasonably, really!

We passed towering Mount Eisenhower (named after President Eisenhower, when he was general of the armies) looking just like a turreted castle, and indeed, it previously had been named, aptly, Castle Mountain. (Why should the name of natural wonders be changed from one given in the past?) It was a delightful scenic drive. Moose grazing in clearings scampered off into the forest at the sound of the car. The only non-pleasant thing was that it had clouded over and there was some light rain.

Much has been written in glowing terms about Lake

Louise, set amid mountains at an altitude of five thousand, six hundred and eighty feet, guarded by the famous Victoria Glacier; we thought we might be disappointed. There are many other lakes in the vicinity, but these could only be reached on foot or by pack-horse; signposts indicated the trails which led to them.

What motels there were were discreetly tucked away from the highway in the village of Lake Louise, a mere cluster of buildings situated a mile distant from the lake. Jeff swung into the large carpark, empty except for two cars. It had stopped raining and the sun broke through.

"No village here, that's why it isn't commercialised," I remarked as we neared the lake on foot.

"The place is probably grossly over-rated."

It was not. It was heavenly! An anonymous poet has said of it:

>(God) 'wished it near, that sometimes He might show
>The saints above His masterpiece below?'

'Lake Louise is of another world' . . . and . . . 'In the lake, ever changing, is Beauty herself, as nearly visible to mortal eyes as she may ever be.' wrote the English poet, Rupert Brooke, when he visited the place in 1913.

Remote Victoria Glacier glistening in the sun was reflected, a white pyramid, in the lake, on each side of which mountains go steeply down, enclosing the expanse of green water on three sides by towering walls of rock. The first white man to discover it was Tom Wilson, in 1881. He called it Emerald Lake, a good description, but three years later it was renamed in honour of one of Queen Victoria's daughters. (Why? What had she done to alert the world to this beauty?)

There were not many people about; we nearly had this splendour to ourselves. The famous, creamy-white hotel, Chateau Lake Louise, with banks of firs rising in crowded growth behind it, which overlooks the lake, had not yet opened for the summer season. It, like the Banff Springs Hotel (which, also, was open for only three months of the year) was a million-dollar establishment run by Canadian Pacific Railways. It was not until 1885 that the railway went west of Banff, giving those who could afford these hotels, accessibility to the marvels of nature.

Clouds were gathering again. We retreated to the car for a picnic lunch, thanking our lucky stars that we had viewed the scene in sunlight. We were quite dazzled by the beauty of it and wished we could stay longer to explore further; there was so much more we would like to have seen. Our afternoon drive would take us into the heart of the Rockies. We knew the road, a narrow, dirt track, might be dangerous in places, with the risk of their being little other transport if anything should befall us.

"I'll be much happier when we reach Golden."

"It's only fifty-seven miles away," I answered with a confidence I certainly did not feel.

The car wheels disturbed the surface of the road causing great clouds of fine dust to billow and rise into the air, where it hung like a smoke screen. We let out a whoop of sheer joy! Ahead was The Great Divide. Beyond that was British Columbia! Two wooden uprights, one each side of the narrow track supported a crossbeam of timber on which, as we approached, we could read 'Alberta'. We passed underneath. Jeff pulled the car into the side.

"Have to have a snap here."

We walked back. The crossbeam now read 'British Columbia'.

"Relax Jeff," I said, looking into the viewfinder at him under the sign.

"I am," he retorted scowling, still standing stiffly like someone about to click his heels in salute. He, himself, is a good photographer, but how he changes when he is on the other side of the lens. He trusts nobody. He faces the camera as though it were a firing squad.

We were in Yoho National Park, five hundred and seven square miles on the west slopes of the Rockies. Yoho! is an Indian exclamation of wonder and delight. Wonderful it really was. Near Field a wide section of road at river level enabled us to pull up safely to take some film of the marvellous scenery. Rock strewn water separated us from the small town. Along the edges of the mountains on the far side of the river a trans-continental train wound its way like a great, grey snake. (We had seen pictures of trains in the Rockies with the engine and tail-end parallel with each other, but on different levels, about four sections of track apart, and the rest of it squiggling back and forth on the intervening rails on the switchback. At the beginning of the century ten thousand men had worked for two years making tunnels through the mountains and laying the tracks for this railway. There had been many appalling accidents and much loss of life.) Loud and piercing on the still air the train's hooter screamed shrilly, one short whistle, followed by a long one; then a bell donged on a single, melancholy note like a church bell tolling for a funeral. Again and again the mountains threw back the sound in mocking echo. Here was something moving, I thought, recalling Ben's advice not to wag the camera about, or pan too often; "If you want motion in your pictures keep the camera steady and film people walking, or moving objects." Thus far I hadn't any opportunity to film anything but stationary mountains; here was a chance to add variety and interest to the masterpiece.

I set the dial on the camera to give the correct exposure, I hoped. (Later, we rued our meanness in not having bought a separate light meter, which would have eliminated guesswork, but funds hadn't stretched that far.) I remembered to wind fully the little arm on the side in preparation for taking a long sequence — I didn't want the motor to run down halfway through. Setting the camera on the tripod, I checked that the head was moving smoothly. Everything in order, I pressed the lever and carefully took aim, following the train. I rewound the motor; took shots of the mountains, the river, and with the telephoto lens some close-ups of the engine, a carriage here and there, some icy peaks on the near mountains, a group of splendid pines, boulders in the water. On projecting the film, imagine my disappointment on viewing the long, long piece of total blackness on our screen: I had forgotten to remove the lens' cap!

The dusty track wound on through ever-more spectacular scenery, considered to be among the most beautiful in the world, frequently inciting us to yell a few 'yohos' ourselves. There was too much to admire, impossible to see it all and, at times, we felt quite overwhelmed. Mountains rising to prodigious heights on all sides, range upon range, crowded in on us. We drove deeper into them. The tortuous road was often barely a car's width, with snow lying in many places where the sun never penetrated. At times, great chunks of ice lay on the track having parted company with a mountain slope – on 1st of June!

On one side rose a sheer wall of rock; on the other there was a precipitous drop to the turbulent waters of the Kicking Horse River. It required the utmost skill and concentration on Jeff's part to drive along this ledge – there were no complaints of boredom today. Alas! he didn't see much of the stupendous surroundings from his crouched position, hands gripping the steering-wheel, now pulling to the right, back to the left, quickly right again, then a long pull to the left, as he negotiated an unexpected extra sharp bend. The road zigzagged dizzily. We could see ahead for only a few yards at a time, never knowing when we reached the corner in view, if we would then turn left or right.

From my seat I saw all the marvels, though not all my breathless gasps were ones of delight! Very often they were suppressed expressions of horror at the narrowness of our excapes from doom. We bounced along, all the boxes in the back noisily jostling each other, the car on one side slithering past the rock walls. Gazing upwards I was unable to see the summits of these rocky monsters. After rounding a bend, in place of the wall of rock there was – nothing. Nothing, until I cast my eyes down to the yawning valley, and always the wheels of the car passing close to the edge of the precipice.

Occasionally the road widened. Whenever it was possible we stopped and got out to revel. In the distance the mountains looked like one continuous range. Nearer ones looked black and ominous with thier rugged snow-capped peaks reaching heavenwards; some were green with trees; others stark.

The road carved along the edge of the mountains, seeming but a thread and winding so sharply that it was impossible to follow it with the eye for any distance, was the only link with civilisation. A sobering thought! Ravines and crevices among the rocks were piled with snow, startlingly white; foaming waterfalls tumbled angrily down mountainsides.

A typical Canadian town we passed through
in British Columbia.

Stanley Park, Vancouver.
With North Vancouver in the background.

Lions Gate Bridge, Vancouver.

Brian at four weeks old.

Brian's Christening, 8th September 1957.
The lady in the flowery hat!

Mavis, Brian and Jeff.
The photograph especially taken to send home.

In Vancouver — when we felt the urge (only slight) to *see* snow, we took a jaunt to Seymour Mountain Park.

Jewel-like lakes, liquid light sparkled amid the beauty of the valleys, swathed in evergreens and hung with glaciers, reaching down. It was breathtaking! Exhilarating! Marvellous! The road wound on, now diving downhill, the car on its nose; now climbing steeply, aiming for the sky. I could gaze in nervous wonder down, down, to a deep valley; within a few minutes we would have descended those thousands of feet and be back at rushing water level again. Up and down, backwards and forwards, until the constant switchbacking made me feel ill.

The new highway, a section of the Trans-Canada, was being blasted through the mountains and from time to time we were flagged to a halt. Perched precariously on the rocky ledge, feeling very vulnerable, we would sit subdued for a minute or two. Then, with a deafening roar, that echoed and re-echoed round the valleys, dynamite exploded loosening great blocks of rock, which came clattering down — sometimes missing the car by yards — to tumble over the edge. In the eerie silence which ensued we would look at one another, surprised to find that we were still alive! Enveloped in a cloud of dust and smoke, like a demon's arrival on a theatre stage, a construction worker would wave us on. After a number of these delays we became blasé — well, almost! — and would continue our journey, as though nothing more than traffic lights set at red had kept us stationary.

Deep in the heart of the mountains the rivers became more numerous. The hazard of traversing these was added to the other nerve-racking experiences already encountered.

"We don't have to go over *that*, surely?" I exclaimed in horror, when I first sighted one of these wooden structures, I'll call a 'bridge'.

"We do," Jeff answered quietly, his very quietness suggesting that he, too, acknowledged that this trip was more than a pleasure jaunt. We were high in the mountains and, though the road was ever-tortuous, we seldom descended to river level; the torrents had to be crossed by these rickety bridges, many were quite long and at times suspended eighty or ninety feet above the water. We would bump around a series of hairpin bends, a steep climb upwards, followed by a ride downhill, then Jeff would negotiate a bridge. My anxiety increased at each attempt. The panoramic view was fantastic, but I was unable to be appreciative. I sat rigid, holding my breath, my heart trying to make a getaway through my ribs. I would breathe a silent prayer when we approached a wooden span, hanging it seemed in mid-air – some bore warnings not to venture across in vehicles over a certain weight – and Jeff would edge the car on, the wheels making a hollow sound, to coax it gently along the creeking boards, the bridge sometimes swaying, and on to the mountain track on the other side. The slats had spaces – too wide for my liking – between them and through these I looked down in quaking terror at waters churning over jagged rocks and pictured a fate worse than death! ('. . . Kicking Horse River . . . a wide, roaring, gushing mass of water . . . greyish green . . .' I wrote in my diary, afterwards – not at the time, I was too petrified to move.)

Two steel bridges were already in place. Now, these form part of the new Trans-Canada Highway and there are no other bridges; instead, the present road, a wonderful feat of engineering, takes a different route than we had to follow. Some sections of road through the Rockies cost one million dollars per *mile* when it was constructed in the 1960s.

We had a couple of narrow escapes. On one occasion in the distance we could see a construction party engaged in blasting operations. A giant bulldozer (from where had it come to get this far into the mountains?) blocked the road ahead. Well back, Jeff drew to a halt, even though we had not been warned to do so. There was no sign of a man with the familiar red flag.

"Wonder how long we'll have to sit here. There's no hope of passing that."

By way of answer to his question the bulldozer shuddered to life and began to move – backwards in our direction. Nearer and nearer it trundled, its driver obviously unable to hear the sounding of our horn. The road was narrow owing to what seemed to be a recent landslide; if Jeff had got out he might have disappeared from this world. On my side it was impossible to open the door at all so tightly wedged were we to the rock face. The back end of the great hulk continued to approach menacingly. The distance grew less between us.

Surely it must stop soon for where could it go . . . he must know he is nearing the end of the straight section? . . . could he round a bend in reverse in that thing? Still it came nearer. We sat frozen by fright. The seconds ticked away. Then a miracle! With but a few yards to spare the driver saw us and braking hard, stopped. Whew!

Moving forward again he pulled in close to the mountain on a piece of road that was just wide enough to let us pass. The driver descended. Although some minutes had elapsed since our near-entry to eternity we were all still very shaken.

"You guys sure gave me a turn; didn't expect anyone on this doggone road."

How did he think we felt?

Not even in the Rockies could we escape that ominous word: detour. Because of the construction of the new highway, the existing road, such as it was, had been closed in places and alternative routes, though short, were frequently hazardous. On occasions we got very little warning of a detour and would round a bend and have to brake hard before pulling away in a different direction from the one we had expected. One time, the small sign marked 'detour' indicated a steep incline — a gulley had been filled in with rubble and sand. We came upon it suddenly. Jeff, in his surprise, hesitated momentarily in getting down to first gear. We climbed slowly. Then, horrors, the car stalled. It began to slide backwards. This is it, I thought. Not a chance! But I underestimated his wonderful control over the car. He slammed on the brakes and applied the handbrake. Mercifully, considering the heavy load in the back, it checked the spinning wheels. After some harrowing moments, with clever manoeuvring on his part, he coaxed the car up the incline to the top and shortly the detour led back to the mountain track. "Hope there's no more like that," Jeff breathed with relief. We both had the jitters.

The sky became overcast; it grew cooler, Cloud softened the outlines of distant mountains; but the near ones were dark and unfriendly with jagged peaks. By this time I was thoroughly exhausted, as much by the surfeit of our splendid surroundings, as by the constant bumping and zigzagging of the car.

No longer able to sit still, I started my usual contortions like a dog chasing his tail, trying to get into a comfortable position to relieve my aches. Jeff looked strained. It had been a gruelling time for him. He had once mentioned self-mockingly, that a teenage ambition of his had been to become a racing driver. His concentration, skill, control, speed of manoeuvre, quick thinking and timing on that journey through the Kicking Horse Canyon was a convincing display of the qualities needed for that profession.

We were too tired to talk. The track widened to become a real road, still gravel, but there were some straight sections. The rivers ceased racing; they were sluggish and broken by islands, many of them wooded. There were a couple more detours; a few more rickety bridges, low-slung not high, and then, just two hours after entering it, we left Yoho National Park. It had been an exhilarating drive. This area of the Rockies is described as 'possessing some of the most spectacular scenery in the world'. I wouldn't disagree!

A dusty road led us into the sleepy town of Golden, a mining and lumber centre, nestling amid mountains on the banks of the Columbia River, only fifty-seven miles from Lake Louise, yet it had taken us nearly three hours to travel it. We booked into a motel: separate cabins, under a stand of pines. Rather sparsely furnished, the main room was dominated by a large, high, chintz-covered bed. Without any delay, kicking off my shoes, I clambered aboard. From my horizontal position, through the open door I could see the car. What a spectacle! It was covered in a layer of grey dust, with here and there bumps of dried, reddish, Ontarian mud showing through; not a hint of blue paint anywhere. Jeff carried in the cases, dumping them heavily on the floor.

"My arms ache," he said.

"Bet they're full of dust."

He threw back the lids. "Not too bad," he replied, "but just look at the car, it's awful!"

"I know. I can see it from here."

"I want to fix the bonnet; the catch is slipping. We need groceries. Will you get them?"

"Yes. All right. Let me recover a little first. It's just after four o'clock."

I dozed briefly; then groaning inwardly, got up and slipped my feet into my sandals. My head spun. I felt wretched.

"Hang on a minute," Jeff said, when he saw I was ready to leave. "I'm just finishing here. We can go together." He banged the bonnet of the car closed. "Might as well walk, will do us good to stretch our legs," he said cheerily.

I did not answer. I felt more like a stretcher-case than an energetic hiker, but he was right I *did* need the exercise. We crossed the bridge over the Columbia River and walked the short distance into town. Golden, somehow, didn't suit it — not when we saw it, anyway. It was oppressive, the sky overcast; everywhere dusty. However, the friendly people in the small, old-fashioned stores more than compensated for its lack of colour. They appeared contented with life; yet in winter the town must be isolated from the outside world. Maybe its inhabitants like it that way. Civilisation can have disadvantages.

In the evening we sat outside the cabin reliving our day's journey, a breeze kept the mosquitoes at bay. Was it really only that morning that we had left Banff? We seemed to have been travelling in mountain terrain for an age. Jeff's twenty-fifth birthday drew to a close. Not a day he, or I, is ever likely to forget.

**Chapter Thirteen**

Again, I was up and dressed before six-thirty *and* I was affable, much to Jeff's amusement.

"Don't worry," I said in answer to his taunting, "when we get settled in Vancouver, I'll revert to my habitual abhorrence of early rising." (I had no experience of babies' habits then!) We drove to the church for eight o'clock Mass. Even the birds were quiet; 'a silence more musical than any song', wrapped itself around the village. A priest in the familiar brown robes of the Order of Saint Francis, was standing on the gravel sidewalk outside the tiny church.

"Good morning," he said. "I don't think I know you?" he asked hesitatingly, thinking that maybe he *should* have known us.

We assured him that we had not met previously. He looked beyond us to our old Dodge, his face registering surprise at seeing it laden with our clobber; to say nothing of the appearance of the car itself, with missing hub caps, smashed light and daubed all over with caked mud, but he made no comment. He came from Eastern Canada he told us. His parishioners were scattered over a mountainous area; some living too far from the church for frequent attendance; therefore, despite the paucity of number, he had a busy life trying to keep in touch with his far-flung flock.

"It's pretty difficult in winter getting about; we are more or less cut off by snow here."

"You must feel very lonely then, Father?" I said.

He did not reply, but his serene demeanour spoke volumes. Was a mountain village in the Rockies much different from the Umbrian hillside in Italy, where the founder of his order had lived believing in the harmony between the Almighty and all of His creation?

It was time for Mass. With a smile, the sort that stays with you all day, he bade us farewell, wishing us a safe journey to Vancouver.

Shafts of sunlight streaming through narrow windows lit the church, gilding the polished sheen on wooden floor and furniture, and throwing the twinkling altar vessels into prominence. I could not help wondering how much help he got in maintaining the church. No doubt like most priests, worldwide, in out-of-the-way communities, he would do his own housework and cooking. It was hard to believe that it was only a week since we had been in the little church in North Bay, Ontario.

We drove out of town along the narrow, bumpy, dusty, gravel road that was Highway 1, the Trans-Canada. In the shade of some trees we had a picnic breakfast of fruit juice, ham and hardboiled eggs. I switched on the dashboard radio. There was a slight pause, before an announcer's voice said, "This is the BBC's General Overseas Service; here is the news." It was 9 am with us, 5 pm in Britain. The London accent prompted nostalgia. What would we have been doing there on a Sunday afternoon? Instead, here we were sitting in a decrepit car, eating a cold breakfast on a deserted stretch of road in British Columbia. If our friends in Dublin and London, could see us . . .

Our next overnight stop would be at Revelstoke. As the crow flies (lucky crows!) it's only a short distance from Golden to Revelstoke, but by road it was two hundred miles, all because some mountains got in the way. Within a few years great road tunnels would penetrate these mountains then man, emulating the crafty crow, could journey by a shorter route; but as we ate our roadside breakfast the mountains formed an impenetrable barrier and we had no option but to follow the Big Bend Highway, part of the Trans-Canada, a giant two hundred mile hairpin bend, a great curve through the Selkirks Mountains, scene of the 1865 Gold Rush. We did not see any gold, only common dust — in our eyes, up our noses, in our clothes, in the car, in the cases . . . We were travelling a dry, sand road in the broad valley of the Columbia River. There were still mountains to be seen in all directions, some wooded, others white, but they didn't hustle us threateningly. They gave us no gasp-making experiences! For the most part we drove through forest, which obscured our view of them. Leafy trees, mainly birch and aspen, mingled with evergreens, at times grew high on one side of the road, low on the other. Jeff's face, which often had been set in taut lines of concentration, looked relaxed.

In a full day's driving we were overtaken by one car and passed six travelling in the opposite direction — not a busy route! After each car passed a pall of dust hung in the air for many minutes. On the Big Bend's two hundred miles of gravel road, there were three service stations, but no habitation whatsoever in between. Shortly after noon, at Lake Kinbasket, ninety-three miles from Golden, at the first of these stations, Esso, we stopped for petrol before going into the restaurant of the adjoining lodge. We were the only people in the sun-filled, glass-enclosed dining-room. A friendly woman chatted, asking us the usual questions, registering the usual surprise at our answers, while she prepared our lunch — there wasn't a lot on offer. The place was open just for a few months during the summer. "The Big Bend Highway closes in the Fall," she told us. "Nobody lives along it then," (there weren't many now!) "We move elsewhere."

Afterwards, we strolled to the lake to stand on the sandy shore, the golden span of water stretching away under the dome of deep blue. An eagle, wings almost motionless, made slow circles for some minutes over a stand of nearby trees, before suddenly dropping like a stone out of sight. He had his lunch, too! The mountains to our west looked like one continuous range with many peaks snow-capped and ribbons of ice running down like streamers. With the sun warm on my face, a slight breeze ruffling my hair I could have stayed for ever. But we didn't, just for twenty minutes or so.

Seven miles further on we passed through Boat Encampment, a small settlement of summer cottages and a filling station perched on the top of the hairpin equidistant from

Golden and Revelstoke. What an ideal spot to have a summer retreat. (A camp was established here in 1811 by a fur trader and explorer, at a point where two trails crossed, one of which led on to the Oregon Trail.) The road crossed the Columbia River there. From then on we drove with the wide river to our right, parallel with the road and never very far from it.

(Many of the places we passed through on this trip would change with the passage of time, but The Big Bend has disappeared. Literally! The building of two dams [Mica and Revelstoke] raised the level of the river, flooding much of the valley. The new Trans-Canada road, high in the mountains, not low in the valley as the Big Bend was for most of its two hundred miles, connects the two points of the hairpin, cutting through a mountain range. The once mighty Columbia River has become a series of lakes and reservoirs. How sad!)

It became increasingly overcast, the heat more oppressive.

"Looks like a thunderstorm brewing," I said.

" 'Fraid so . . . nothing like variety: we have had a snowstorm and a dust-storm already on this trip."

"And a thunderstorm, remember, in Northern Ontario?"

"Oh yes, I'd forgotten . . . well we're going to have more thunder and there's plenty of dust about today, but we should make it to Vancouver before the snow season starts."

Some thirty minutes later an earsplitting bang accompanied by a series of sharp bumps announced, not the beginning of a thunderstorm, but a puncture in one of the back tyres.

"Damn!" Jeff said with annoyance, quickly reversing the car into a grassy clearing in the trees, "Why did this have to happen?"

I curbed the instinct to point out that we had covered 2,600 miles without serious incident; climbing out of the car I sent aloft a prayer of thanks that it hadn't occurred on yesterday's journey through The Kicking Horse Pass or indeed, on any number of bad sections of road we had encountered.

We were at river level and through the trees I caught glimpses of the great Columbia sweeping south. For the first time in days there wasn't a sign of a mountain; they were obscured by the intervening forest and dense undergrowth. The lush grass at my feet was a startling green. There was a pervasive smell of mint.

"Whew! It's hot." I complained, making for shelter.

"Not there for heaven's sake. Bears!" Jeff called from his crouching position at the rear of the car.

How stupid of me! We had read several warnings along the way advising the carrying of fire-arms if leaving the road. Grizzly as well as black bear roamed in this area. I peered into the undergrowth half-expecting to be confronted by a pair of eyes watching me, but on a sultry afternoon a bear would have more sense than we had, and would be resting, with any luck!

There were many wooden bridges over tributaries, but although the road was undulating in places, mercifully, these bridges were all at river level; there was no repetition of the previous day's anxiety. In the space of an hour, travelling in the opposite direction, three cars, of the six that we saw all day, passed us.

"Don't like driving on crowded roads," Jeff joked.

It grew darker. There was an uncanny stillness. On the sandy surface, the big drops at first caused eddies of dust where they plopped, but the rain grew steadily heavier until it was falling in straight, grey sheets, blotting out the verdant surroundings, quickly turning the road to mud. The downpour on the car roof made a terrific din, while the wipers flicked furiously at the stream of water coursing down the windscreen. After twenty minutes the rain ceased. But it had not cleared the oppressiveness; on the contrary the humidity was worse.

"Is this a man?" Jeff asked, incredulously.

I followed his gaze and saw coming towards us, walking briskly in the centre of the road, head bent, small bundle Dick-Whittington-style over his right shoulder . . . a man! Had he been a Martian we couldn't have been any more flabbergasted.

"Where can he be heading?"

Without looking in our direction or altering pace he moved over to the side of the road and, eyes downcast, strode purposefully past. We didn't call out to him. Obviously he did not wish to acknowledge us. Maybe he *was* a Martian!

The green jungle to our left grew less dense, letting in mountain views again. We stopped to have a drink. I took the opportunity to take some movie film of the Monashee Range.

"I'm awfully hungry," Jeff complained, flexing and stretching his arms and massaging his wrists. "My arms are still paining from yesterday's drive. What food have we got?"

"Not much," I replied, more interested in film than food just then. Low mutterings about incompetent housekeepers accompanied his scavenging in the grocery box.

In the interest of assuaging his hunger we pulled up in Downie Creek, a tiny settlement, the only one, on the hundred-mile stretch between Boat Encampment and Revelstoke. Here, there wasn't much available either. We had to make do with large portions of home-made apple pie and tea.

Smoke rising among the trees was the first indication we had that a section of the forest, through which we were travelling, was on fire. It was some distance away, but when we drew nearer the smoke thickened and heat waves made the air dance. Tackling the blaze with hoses, which snaked across the dirt road carrying water from the Columbia, there were fire-fighters attired in helmets and heavy boots. Flames flickering, wood crackling, when we were waved on, we drove slowly over the hoses, then picked up speed to get clear of the place swiftly.

As always, by this time of the day I was tired and aching. Revelstoke must be close now, I consoled myself. Yes, Revelstoke was close, but that didn't mean that we would reach it soon, or that the remaining few miles would be uneventful.

The morning sun long vanished, the sky grew menacing, the heat more stifling.

"It's going to be the mother and father of a storm when it does break," I said.

"Hope we get to Revelstoke before it starts. It's difficult enough driving on this winding road when the surface is dry," Jeff added.

We rounded a bend and were very surprised to see a car in a semi-circular clearing on our left. A woman and a couple of children were sitting on a rug on the grass.

"Good, we must be near civilisation . . . they look like locals just spending the day here."

On passing them, Jeff noticed a pair of grey-flannelled legs; the rest of the body was obscured by the raised bonnet of the car.

"Better see if he needs help," he said, forgetting his gnawing hunger in his concern to act the good Samaritan.

"Suppose so," I agreed, reluctantly, being quite prepared to pass 'on the other side', feeling more sorry for myself than charitable towards others.

Jeff crossing the clearing on foot, spoke to the man for a moment or two and returned to me.

"The petrol pump isn't working. It shouldn't take long to fix it. Do you want to stay here or sit with the others on the grass?"

"Here. I'm much too tired to make polite conversation."

"Won't be long."

Time dragged. The sky grew more threatening. From time to time I felt that, for the sake of good manners, I ought to go over to speak to the woman, but exhaustion overcame any pangs of conscience. It was after six — almost an hour had passed. The elements activated decision. A jagged streak of lightning ripped apart the clouds. Simultaneously there was a tremendous roll of thunder. Before the echoes had died away there was another flash, another boom. Rain poured in torrents. Surely Jeff would return now? The woman shooed the children into the car; dumped her belongings into the boot and scrambled into her seat. The two men remained stooped over the car; their drenched shirts plastered to their skin. I was greatly relieved when Jeff approached.

"No luck in getting him moving." He brushed the back of an oily hand across his streaming forehead leaving black streaks on his wet face, his dark hair stuck in little curls to his head. "I'll have to push them," he said.

"*Push* them! Oh no, Jeff, please don't! Not in this . . . "

"No problem. I'll push them," he said with his usual confidence, as one might contemplate helping a friend in a quiet suburban road. "It's not far to Revelstoke. Anyway their engine will probably pick up when we get moving."

We drove across and got behind them, tucking our front

bumper into their rear one. Slowly he edged the other car forward on to the once-sandy-now-muddy road. The other car manoeuvred until safely placed in the middle of the track, but ours overshot. Jeff braked hard. On my side, the road fell away to the valley below shrouded in rain.

"That was close," Jeff said, tersely.

I didn't answer, only thanked God for sparing us yet again! I was trembling all over.

In tandem, carefully we rounded several bends without further incident; then the other car spluttered into life to travel along independently. "Told you so," Jeff remarked, vindicated. The driver waved in salute through his window.

The storm grew quieter; the rain thinned; surrounded by mountains, directly beneath us was Revelstoke. A steep run down and we were there. The driver indicated with his hand that we were to follow him. He drove through the town to the outskirts on the other side before pulling up outside adjoining bungalows built well back from the roadway. We all piled out.

"Come and have cawfee," the lady offered. "It was ver' good of you to take such trouble to help. You sure gave us a fright . . . thought you were goin' over that cliff. Were you scared?" she asked me, eyeing me up and down, blatantly surprised.

Of course I was scared! There was much to be scared about — in truth, ever since arriving in Canada I had been scared of something or other. Apart from anything else, expecting one's first baby, though exciting, is, also at times, a scary experience for most women, I imagine . . . a mere man couldn't comprehend that. It seemed to me that Jeff didn't understand fear or self-doubt; his apparent self-confidence sometimes borders on arrogance. He explains this attitude by saying that he undertakes only that which he feels he can achieve with success. Maybe. But I consider that a saying of my grandmother's has some influence, too — 'The devil looks after his own!'

A long flight of stone steps led up to the heavy, entrance door. While she bustled in the kitchen, he, plump with pride because he had done most of the construction himself, showed us around the bungalow. The interior was not yet finished: a couple of rooms had bare plaster walls and unpainted woodwork.

"Ready?" his wife called. I beheld the dining-table. When she had suggested we should stay for 'cawfee', she meant just that, unless a plate of dainty cookies could be termed food. We struggled to control our stomach rumbles.

They were Germans. "I own all this land," he explained, gesturing through the window at a wide area of grass. "I bought it cheaply before the war. I'll sell it for building, when the price is right."

They had been in residence for only a short time, having moved from the next-door bungalow where "the windows were too low; they got snowed over in winter. When we built this, we made sure to place the windows above snow level."

"What depth of snow do you get?" I asked amazed, remembering the long flight of steps outside.

"Oh 'bout nine feet," he said matter-of-factly.

"*Nine feet!*"

They laughed at our consternation. "You get used to it," they assured us. (Revelstoke has the greatest snowfall of any town on the five-thousand-mile Trans-Canada Highway.)

"Have you no windows lower than nine feet above ground?"

"No. We rely on air-conditioning in the basement."

And we were escaping from Toronto because of its snow. To these folk, Toronto would seem like the tropics.

"In winter you must be cut off?"

"Yes, often, the Big Bend is closed, of course, but the highway running west is usually open. We love it here. We have marvellous ski slopes; people come from all over Canada, from the States, too."

Chacun a son gout! There is no accounting for taste. But considering how Revelstoke has developed as a winter sports region, I bet he made a tidy profit on the sale of his land.

Jeff explained about our puncture and that he needed to have the tyre fixed. There was nowhere open at that time on a Sunday evening, but our friend knew a garage owner.

"I'll see what I can do. I'll go along with you."

The tyre would be repaired by morning. He then booked

us into a motel, paying the charge, before thanking Jeff for his help and wishing us a safe journey to the coast.

'The Rest of your Days Depends on the Rest of your Nights', read a billboard advertisement at the entrance to the motel. It was a group of separate units with housekeeping (cooking) facilities, each resembling a miniature log cabin, among evergreens, a distance from the road — all very restful and picturesque; however, we were in no mood for eulogising. We were famished. At 9 pm a small grocery store, with a coffee bar, was all we could find open; the only food available to stifle our hunger pangs: sandwiches. We bought bacon, sausages, eggs, bread and milk. They would make a substantial breakfast, because, on returning to the motel, we were too exhausted to cook them!

The chintz on the window kept the room dark, but through the uncurtained panel above the door in the corner, I could see that the sky was already lightening; and from the trees all around the dawn chorus racketed to greet the new-born day. What a cacophony! I have never heard such a row. It was twenty past four. Eventually, I drifted back to sleep.

"Come on, wake up!" Jeff said. "It's 7.30 am."

"I was awake hours ago."

"Oh yes! Sleep hasn't diminished my appetite. What about breakfast? By the way take a look inside the cases. Someone has dumped a lump of the Sahara in them — there's more dust than clothes." There was dust in everything, even in the pockets of folded shirts.

While the bacon and sausages sizzled, we carried the table and chairs on to the porch. It was already warm. Revelstoke may be a famous winter resort, a place of brilliant skies, glistening mountains and colourful skiers; but I am content to remember the town on that glorious, June morning, while we ate in the shade, the air heady, morning mist floating around the mountains like gossamer, the piquancy of pine mingled with the aroma of bacon and coffee. Gorgeous!

We collected the repaired wheel from the garage when they opened; filled up with gas and soon after nine hit the trail for another day. The mist lifted. The sun transmuted the snowy mountain tops to molten gold. There were some bad patches of gravel, an uneven surface, but dry. Alongside Mara

Lake, loggers felling trees had brought down a monster, which blocked the roadway delaying us for fifteen minutes, the first of many stops for similar reasons that day; we occupied ourselves by filming the lake.

The surroundings — as always in British Columbia — were marvellous, the startling emerald reminding us of Ireland; "The result of abundant rain in both places," we agreed ruefully. But there were no clouds about today, thank goodness. I wrote in my notebook, 'Since crossing into British Columbia I have felt at home for the first time since arriving in Canada.' It must have been the lushness, the vividness of the green and the soft air, which reminded me of Ireland because, of course, the physical features of the place are on a gigantic scale compared with home. The trees were different too. And different from those east of the Rockies. The mountains not only cut off British Columbia from the rest of Canada, but, along with the Pacific Ocean, they also influence the climate and consequently the vegetation. The pines, larches, hemlocks have an eastern and a western variety. Here, also, there were truly giant red cedars and along the lakes I noticed pine trees with extraordinary long needles, which I later found out were called Ponderosa pine and those long needles are very sharp.

Waterways were crossed by narrow, wooden bridges. The mountains were clothed in green and less rugged now. It surprises me to learn that some dislike this scenery, claiming that they feel overpowered, confined by it; they prefer gentle undulating countryside or the flat prairies with the freedom afforded by infinite space; but we loved it from the moment we passed through The Great Divide in Yoho National Park. We felt sure we were doing the right thing in moving to Vancouver; the tricky part of the journey over, all we had to do was follow the highway to the coast.

"We'll be there tomorrow," I said with delight. Wrong! Very wrong!

Highway 1 continues through Kamloops and down the Fraser Canyon to Hope; but we wanted to see something of the famed Okanagan Valley; therefore, just short of Salmon Arm, we said good-bye to Highway 1, which we had followed for two thousand miles — *two thousand miles* across four provinces — since leaving Nipigon, turned left and took route 97 south.

Milk churns in groups at gateways along the road, thousands of haystacks in fields, seemingly endless acres of orchards and nurseries were proof of the fertile, farming land of the Okanagan. I believe in springtime, when millions of fruit trees are in blossom the fragrant beauty of the entire valley is indescribable, yet only a century earlier the first experiments in fruit growing had been made by a missionary, a Father Pandory.

We passed through Vernon on Woods Lake, a pleasant town. The locality, famous for its fish, also offered then a varied selection for the huntsman from grouse to black or grizzly bear. (Alas! nowadays bears exist in greatly diminished numbers.) The road, with a couple of viewpoints, ran high above Lake Kalamalka, which means the lake of many colours.

The wooded hills were reflected in the expanse of water, shaded from delicate turquoise to sombre green, owing to the altering configuration of the lake bottom, also light and angle; but how much more romantic to imagine that something magical caused the various colours. Some ambulance planes at anchor bobbed up and down.

"We're nearing Ogopogoland," Jeff said.

A strange denizen called Ogopogo, akin to the Loch Ness monster, and just as elusive, is sighted in Lake Okanagan at intervals, but he is wary of cameras . . . We didn't see him, anyway! The road ran roughly parallel with the lake, but some distance from it; we did not see much of it until we neared Kelowna. The town was famous for its regatta held annually for four days in August, it also handled the marketing of produce from the vast Okanagan Valley. Route 97 crossed the lake by government car-ferry and continued south along the west shore. (How Kelowna has grown over the years! Today, there is a six-lane highway approach to a bridge, which replaced the ferry.)

At the landing stage we joined a line of waiting cars. Pervading everywhere the spicey smell of pine, we saw new timber stacked in high piles along the dockside. The crossing on the small ferry, costing fifty cents for a car and driver and five cents for each passenger, took fifteen minutes. Boats of every description plied the waterway, and there were a couple of waterskiers enjoying themselves. The countryside all around was very beautiful.

We drove off and on through open country, a startling green after the calm blue-green of the lake. Notices along the roadside warned that Open Range Cattle were at large; a change from Watch Out For Bear signs we had seen on previous days. We pulled off the road to have a late picnic lunch, while listening to Vancouver Radio, thrilled by the fact that we were getting ever nearer our goal.

The small towns we passed through during the afternoon had lovely names: Peachland, Summerland, Trout Creek. Ten miles beyond Penticton, an attractive town situated at the southern tip of long, narrow Lake Okanagan, we turned west on to Highway 3 to Princeton, where we stopped for gas. It had been a pleasant drive and I did not feel any of the awful tiredness I had experienced each day from lunch-time onwards, therefore, I readily agreed to Jeff's proposal of driving to Hope eighty-five miles away. That would leave us just one hundred miles from Vancouver, which we could 'do' in the morning. It would nearly 'do' us first.

We were on a wide sweep of road: the famed Hope-Princeton Highway. 'You will never forget the smooth surface of this wonderful road, never forget this highway . . .' a description in a pamphlet promised us. True. We shall not forget it, but not for the reasons mentioned; it marked the beginning of a series of events which aged us both considerably. Our enjoyable ride lasted a matter of minutes, when several rocking bumps brought us to a halt. Another puncture! It was ludicrous to think it should happen here on one of the most perfect surfaces in the whole of Canada. (A few weeks later we heard on the radio that there had been two fatal accidents within a couple of days at the same spot.) I sat on a grassy bank. Swarms of blackflies flitted about deciding that they liked me very much. Jeff quickly changed the wheel; batting away the horrid, biting, winged creatures we got back into the car.

"That didn't take long," he said turning the starter. Nothing happened. Another couple of turns with no result.

"Think it may be the petrol pump. You'd better get out again." Jeff pulled on his overalls and crawled under the car. "Ouch!" he said, "the road is baking."

There was no protection from the sun; blackflies descended like locusts; then I discovered that I was sitting on an anthill; swatting, flicking, brushing, swiping, perspiration running down my face, near to tears I soon had enough. Further up the road there were some overhanging trees. There was no sidewalk; to avoid the traffic, I walked lopsidedly, one foot up the bank, one in the roadway until I reached the oasis of shade.

Passing motorists had a good view of my antics as balancing awkwardly on the slope I removed one shoe clearing it of ants, then the other, shaking them off my clothes, in between times waving at the flies; the latter had been joined by another flying insect with an even more vicious bite. It was not a fair contest; no matter how quickly I retaliated they dived and swooped and succeeded in stinging me on every inch of uncovered skin.

Poor Jeff! He wasn't having a good time either. He was in and out under the car, getting blacker in looks and mood all the time. One and a half hours later the engine throbbed to life. He turned the car around and we headed back to Princeton. "No hope of getting to Hope today," he said wearily. It was the first time that we had had to double back; just as we thought all the difficult driving was over.

It was seven o'clock when we booked into a motel and without changing or having a shower set off on foot in search of a meal. What a sight – Jeff, apart from his hands, which he *had* washed, covered in oil and grime; I with sunburnt face marked, as were my arms and legs, with ugly weals. Indians call these bloodsucking insects: No-see-ums. They have been known to drive a man – or woman – mad!

There was a flower-festooned porch at the motel, but there were also gnats in their millions; we remained indoors. Sleep came fitfully, the night a long, itching agony. There was no fan. We had the choice of suffocating with just a small window open – the only one with protective netting – or throw open the big window, which I longed to do, and be devoured by marauding mosquitoes.

## Chapter Fourteen

We had breakfast early in an adjacent snack bar. While waiting for the puncture to be repaired, Jeff washed down the car, with limited success. Before long, we were once again on the Hope-Princeton Highway or, to be more accurate for us, on the Princeton-Hope. There were pretty bungalows in lawned gardens with roses and flowers reminding us of home and a gentler climate, and horses in hedged fields, not vast tracts of grassland. Within an hour, we were in the mountains, in Manning Park, with waterfalls tumbling in gorges and although, at times, we were as much as 4,500 feet above sea-level, the climb seemed effortless on such a highway, winding, climbing, dipping, giving us everchanging views. 'The smooth surface' and 'wonderful road' were as the guide-book promised. And we will 'never forget' it . . . alas!

We passed a motel set back from the road in spacious, shaded grounds and ponies in a nearby field. "I suppose those are the ponies used for trail rides," I said.

"Guess so," Jeff replied. "Smashing place to spend a few days. We'll come here with junior sometime. Look over there," he said pointing among the trees, "those kids are quite tiny; see how confidently they sit astride their ponies."

At Allison Pass, we were four and a half thousand feet above sea-level and more than halfway to Hope. Then we came upon a whole hillside of burned-out forest, 6,000 acres; the charred tree stumps marring the beauty of the place. Suspended from a gallows by the road was a huge, dummy cigarette with the words underneath: The Camper Who Dropped This Should Also Be Hanged. Painted in giant letters on the highway and on signs at intervals along the roadside we had read: 'Keep British Columbia Green' and wondered why it had been repeated so frequently. The emphasis on green underlined the hideousness of the graveyard of blackened trees. My protestations about the smoker's carelessness were not endorsed by Jeff; instead he was muttering to himself, "H'm the oil must be running out . . . Fast! Wonder if? . . . there must be . . . a leak!"

At various high level places there were viewpoints, but who would stop to admire the scenery, when the prospect of being stranded in the middle of such splendour was quite possible? In fact, we had eyes for nothing but the oil pressure gauge where the needle flickered ever lower towards zero. Jeff free-wheeled when he could, for four miles on one occasion, and coaxing the car along the winding road, we limped to a service station. (He usually carried a supply of gas and oil, but he must have left the oil can behind, while he was engaged in washing the car that morning.) The oil tank was empty. How lucky we were! I might have had to wait in the car while Jeff went for emergency supplies. someone – not Old Nick, I'm sure! – was looking after us.

Another couple of patches of burned-out woodland and then just after eleven o'clock we arrived in Hope. The main street ran along a great curve of the Fraser River. We called at several garages but nobody could see to the car, to check why it was losing oil, until late afternoon. With a cheekiness born of desperation, Jeff persuaded a proprietor to let him use his garage and tools, if he did the job himself. He found that the problem was a leaking gasket at the petrol pump, which he replaced.

While he was sorting out the car, not wanting to chance a repeat encounter with insects, I had a look around Hope. Whoever named the place could not have foreseen the day we were going to spend there! The town is set in a saucer-shaped valley, with the inevitable mountains all around, six or seven, forming an almost complete circle. The summits were sharply defined, their sides clothed in trees. Lush lawns, abundant flowers and exceedingly tall conifers edged one side of a large square, a pond with a fountain in the grounds of a motel, small shops and pretty bungalows all contributed to an attractive town.

I could feel the sun-baked road hot through my sandals. After an hour, having done a couple of circuits of the place, I returned to the garage. With grateful thanks for the use of the tools, Jeff offered payment, which was declined with: "No! Sure hope it's OK now."

We lunched in town. At the time, Jeff didn't give any clue of his concern, but sometime afterwards he admitted that, at that juncture he began to feel that our previous good luck with the car was about to change; after two punctures and the oil leak happening within a few hours driving, he was wondering what the next problem would be. I was experiencing a mixture of emotions: relief at having got this far, a little over a hundred miles to go to the Pacific, and apprehension about what lay ahead for both of us — for the three of us! — but I didn't voice any of this. Instead, we chatted about what we would do on arrival in Vancouver in about three hours' time. In three hours we would be? . . . still in Hope!

The road out of town began to climb. We were nearing the end of the Fraser Canyon; "Now we just follow the Fraser River to journey's end." Just then we very nearly reached our lives' end. The car engine cut out suddenly, bringing us to a jolting halt. "My God, the baby!" With a screech of brakes the car behind pulled up. A blare of raucous horns added to Jeff's annoyance and did nothing for my nerves. Our car obstinately refused to budge. With its nose skywards, there we were perched a few yards short of a blind corner, a wall of rock to our left, white bollards marking the edge of the side of the road, a mere few feet from us, level with the tops of tall trees, their roots down in the Fraser Canyon. A stream of cars travelled in the opposite direction, while one by one from behind us the drivers pulled out cautiously to overtake, giving a glare when they passed. Seriously, did they think we were sightseeing?

"We'll have to reverse and free-wheel to the bottom," Jeff said. "It must be the petrol pump again."

"Reverse. How?"

"I'll manage," he answered, confidently. "There's a garage not far from here. I saw it when we passed."

It appeared that Hope was the most popular place in Western Canada, because a line of cars came around the corner towards us and down into the town. How Jeff was going to succeed in turning the car, which was facing uphill, without an engine, was beyond my powers of comprehension. Still suffering the shock of the sudden halt, limply, I sat watching the cars whizzing by above the tree-tops.

Sensing my alarm, Jeff said solicitously. "If you are nervous (if!) get out and walk back, I'll see you at the bottom of the hill."

I was quite certain the car would end up at the *bottom* of the Fraser Canyon . . . in which case, I would rather meet our doom together. Anyway, "Get out . . . " was itself suggesting suicide in that traffic.

He proceeded to do a three-point turn in reverse. Drivers passed mouthing, "Goddarn fool," "Idiot," and other endearments! Eventually we coasted down and stopped across the road from a garage the car was pushed into the forecourt. They didn't have a replacement pump. Abandoning me and the car, Jeff hoofed it, about a mile into town. (Our second turning back on our journey in two days.) He returned after an age with a petrol pump and disappeared into the office. Nobody had time to do the job. Once again he borrowed tools and set about it himself. The place was busy and we were very much in the way, but at least we were not evicted.

He donned his overalls; he looked hot and weary. There was nowhere offering shade. I sat in the car with my back to the door; my aching legs along the bench seat. I'll die soon, I thought dramatically, warding off faintness. The yard spun, then righted itself, blacked out and came back into focus again. The pumps receded until they were mere coloured dots, then grew and grew until they were giants with long arms. At last it was time to move off. The boss watched from his office. No effusiveness from this man, good riddance more likely.

Jeff was listening to the engine. "It sounds all right."

Up the hill we went towards that corner. Once there, believe it or not, with a series of choking coughs the car chugged to a standstill.

"Not again!" he exploded, thumping the steering-wheel in annoyance. He cajoled the car — it was always a painfully slow procedure — and we were halfway across, when the engine spluttered momentarily, jolting the car backwards. Hard on the brakes. But there was a delay. The car continued to move. The twenty-inch, white roadside markers stood out against the green treetops. Jeff grabbed the handbrake and the rear of the car touched one of these bollards. The car stopped. A hairsbreath, literally, between us and eternity.

"That was a close shave," he said, in a very wobbly voice.

I was numb with fright. White-faced, but composed, he wrestled with the steering-wheel and the car rolled forward.

Without taking his eyes off the road, he asked, "Are you all right?"

"I think so."

Then we were coasting downhill again, and again, and again: five attempts altogether; each time conking out at that fateful spot. We continued to bolster each other's nerve: to admit difficulties might be akin to admitting defeat. A hundred miles was all that separated us from our goal — we couldn't give in now — but we spent nigh on *four hours* trying to get out of Hope. Its saucer shape surrounded by mountains took on sinister connotations: A Roman amphitheatre with wild beasts? A snakepit?

We would approach the hill with bated breath. Would we make it this time? Would we heck . . . I don't know which I dreaded more, the inescapable stalling, or having to face the mechanics whose reception had long ceased to be friendly. We had cluttered up the garage for hours, using *their* tools, and we hadn't even bought petrol because we had bought it at lunch-time! Jeff got more and more angry with himself for being unable to sort out the problem. For me, with nothing to do but stew and fret in the heat of the car, becoming ever more faint and anxious, the time passed with aching slowness. I prayed that someone would get us out of this mess. Soon!

The sixth attempt: cautiously up the hill, our ears listening for the engine to cut out. It didn't. It didn't. We sailed smoothly around the corner. Dumbfounded! We pictured them back at the garage — the time lag and no sign of us. Maybe the boss would strut across the yard, look up the highway to see if we were coming, nowhere in sight . . . "They've gone, say them guys have gone!" he would call to the others.

"Remember to send them a card from Vancouver." Jeff laughed.

We wondered if we should ask for a tablet to be inlaid in the road bearing the inscription: 'The Gores Stopped Here'. (Months later, Jeff discovered the trouble had been in the gas lines — the rubber lines were closing up because of the heat!)

More gravel road. More road construction. One way traffic. A bulldozer lumbered awkwardly. We were forced to stop. Stop, being the operative word, because when the bulldozer moved to the edge of the road and we were flagged on, the engine refused to pick up. Groans from us; honking horns from others; after an interminable couple of minutes the car jerked to life. We were off.

Each time we had to slow down or stop in traffic, and there *was* light traffic continuously, unlike many of the previous days when there was next to none, we dreaded the consequences, but by coaxing the engine with the choke, cosseting, fussing, like a parent with an obstreperous child, Jeff kept us going at a steady rate, only stalling — and thumping the steering-wheel — twice.

There are miles and miles of scenic, verdant countryside in the Lower Fraser Valley. We passed through lovely Chilliwack, Mount Cheam in the background, not delaying to have a look around in case the car, thinking it had reached journey's end, sat down like a stubborn donkey, and on to Abbotsford where, instead of continuing along Highway 1, which we had rejoined outside Hope, we crossed the River Fraser to Mission City on to the highway running north of the river, which eventually, some thirty-five miles further on, would lead us into Vancouver.

We were both dreadfully thirsty. It was several hours since we had lunch and it was very warm, but we dare not stop. Lush fields slipped away on both sides of the paved, straight road and, as always, in British Columbia there were mountains. The highway became four-laned and busy. We had not seen traffic like this since Winnipeg half a continent, seventeen hundred miles, away! During the day we had gained an hour by crossing a time zone; (we were now on Pacific Time) nevertheless it was six o'clock when we neared Port Moody, fifteen miles east of Vancouver, so we decided to spend the night there and make our triumphant entry into the promised land the next morning. Jeff had trouble restarting the car after stopping for petrol and it stalled again as we drove into the forecourt of a motel.

"Maybe we won't make it to Vancouver," I laughed.

"We will," Jeff answered fervently. "Even if I have to push the car the fifteen miles!"

Later in the evening, when the heat had abated, he worked on it for a couple of hours and I shopped for groceries to save time the next day, leaving us free to find somewhere to live. With the anxiety of the journey over, we would have to face the problem of finding accommodation, which we knew was scarce in Vancouver, but that was for the future. Now we were both quite thrilled to have got this far. By our reckoning, in our circumstances, it had been an epic journey.

"What the car needs is a good rest," Jeff said, on coming inside.

"That goes for us, too," I replied.

Once again beams of sunlight woke me early. I padded through to the living-room, cool and dim after the warm brilliance of the bedroom, to stand at the window. A haze, heralding the heat to follow, shrouded everything beyond the limits of the neat hedge, that bordered the garden. I was filled with joy. Not until that moment had I admitted to myself how frightened I had been, how worried, how full of doubts; I felt all the aching tension draining away to be replaced by a feeling of peace, of hope for our future. My reverie was interrupted.

"What about breakfast?" Jeff asked. "I'll see if the car is all right while you get it ready."

"It's running OK," he said on returning indoors. After the day-long tussle, that was a bonus.

We wrote to our respective parents to let them know we had arrived, although we would have to continue using the

GPO for our mail. Handing back the motel keys, we left Port Moody. Not only was the town named after him, but General Moody was the founder of the *Province* of British Columbia. Many years later, on a visit to St. Peter's Church, the mother church of Bournemouth in the south of England, I saw his grave. The churchyard has many other notables buried there: William Godwin, Mary Wollstonecroft, Mary Shelly (author of *Frankenstein*) and the Romantic Poet Shelley's heart, but I don't think any of them has a town named in their honour.

The fifteen miles from Port Moody were covered speedily.

"Vancouver!" we bellowed on seeing the roadside marker bearing the name. The mileometer showed that we had covered 3,168 miles since leaving Toronto. Not bad going considering the state of many of the roads, to say nothing of the fact that we had spent most of the eleventh day trying to get out of Hope. (Ben had always claimed number eleven was a troublesome one!)

We had a great sense of achievement. Not many people would have travelled the route we had covered — sections of it, yes, but not over three thousand miles, all of it through Canada, in eleven days, in an ancient saloon car with only one driver and a heavily pregnant passenger! We had wanted to see something of Canada and driving through five provinces had shown us the extent of the varied scenery — and weather! — throughout the continent.

It would take another five and a quarter years — thirteen years' construction altogether — to complete the Trans-Canada Highway: the longest paved road in the world! We had travelled approximately two thirds of its overall length, much of it *not* on paved surface. Work began in 1950 to construct a two-lane highway following the shortest and least difficult route through each province. In many places existing roads became part of the cross-continental highway, but for the most part the task of construction was not easy, because it had to be built over muskeg (swamp) wilderness and mountains spread out along the route. We had viewed all this and much more. We felt we had seen billions of trees, thousands of mountains, limitless square miles of prairies as well as muskeg and wilderness, rivers and lakes. And road construction! What an undertaking it was for the road builders. And for us! What a country it is.

We passed the Empire Stadium on our right, built three years previously, in 1954, to host the British Empire Games. A placard at a drugstore read: 'Three in City win on Irish Sweep.' Just like that! You would think that Ireland was around the corner, and not six thousand miles away — the irony of it.

Cream coloured trolley buses were passing up and down. Maybe there were no street-cars? If so, that alone would help me to love the place!

"Must buy a map," Jeff said, pulling up outside a garage. Parked on an incline, wide, straight Hastings Street stretched ahead and down into the sprawling city, its buildings dwarfed by the towering mountains surrounding it, their snowy peaks gilded by sun; Stanley Park, a green peninsula jutting out into the waters of English Bay. Vancouver! The city our baby would call home. Had the risks we had taken been worthwhile? Already I knew the answer.

## Chapter Fifteen

Jubilant at having arrived we were in holiday mood and first called in at the Visitors' Information Centre on the corner of Georgia and Seymour Streets, to pick up some pamphlets — not that we intended to be mere visitors after the effort taken in getting there — then back to Hastings Street to the General Post Office to collect our mail to be chastened on reading it to learn that our parents were worried. Hoping to mollify them, we posted our letters giving details of our safe arrival.

Like a couple of kids on a special outing, we did a tour of the city. Surrounded by snow-capped peaks with the sea at its doorstep, Vancouver, with a population then of 400,000, had an air of lively prosperity, which greatly impressed us. A compact city, it had few high rise buildings. The twenty-one-storied, six-hundred-roomed Vancouver Hotel, operated jointly by Canadian National and Canadian Pacific Railways, and a similar structure, The Marine Buildings, double landmarks overlooking the harbour, were the tallest buildings in the place. We drove through Stanley Park, a thousand acres of primaeval forest, yet only five minutes from the city centre, and crossed The Lion's Gate Toll Bridge, the longest suspension bridge in the Commonwealth, spanning First Narrows at the entrance to the inner harbour, with North Shore Mountain straight ahead, the bridge being the only way, apart from a ferry, to get from Vancouver to North and West Vancouver, because Second Narrows Bridge at that time was under construction. We made a quick tour of newly-opened Park Royal shopping centre — without spending any money, of course — considered to be one of the most elaborate of its kind in Canada. The houses on that side of

English Bay were sparsely scattered in gardens colourful with flowers against a backdrop of wooded mountains, extremely beautiful, quite definitely not in our price range for renting, if there were any for renting!

Paying the toll again, once more we traversed The Lions Gate Bridge (the Lions are two mountain peaks), which afforded a wonderful panoramic view; returned to the city; bought a newspaper; made some telephone calls about apartments and quickly nose-dived, when we realised that pregnancy was regarded like the plague by most landladies and 'sorry no children' (well, expected child) was their catch-cry. Our euphoria at reaching the end of our marathon evaporated somewhat, although our first impressions of Vancouver convinced us that we had done the right thing in coming here.

Cruising in the car on the lookout for overnight accommodation we saw, hanging askew outside a dilapidated house, a scrawled notice: Suite to Let. Suite seemed rather grand for such an establishment, but in Vancouver it was in common usage instead of apartment. Our knock on the door was answered by a chubby girl of about my own age. Very pregnant. Giving me an amused smile, displaying beautiful teeth, she eyed my bulge while explaining that she was a tenant of only a couple of weeks duration; the landlord was indisposed.

"Gee is that your car?" she asked, her eyes standing out like organ stops. "You have Ontario plates?"

"We have come from Toronto."

"From *Toronto*, in *that!*"

The 'suite' consisted of a large, dim room with walls painted drab green. Off it a glass-enclosed balcony served as a kitchenette, pleasantly bright after the living-room, but there was neither sink nor running water. There *was* a gas stove. It didn't seem possible, but there it squatted, the identical twin to the one Eva and Ben had in Toronto – broken plate rack, chipped enamel and all. The rest of the furniture had probably drifted overboard from the ark: vintage stuff; but not the kind of vintage that costs money, more the sort that costs money to have it carted away as rubbish.

"What's that?" Jeff enquired, indicating what appeared to be an enormous heap of dusty clothing.

"That," said the girl, Bonnie, clearing her throat apologetically, is a bed-settee, a bed."

"A bed," we chortled. "How is it a bed? How?"

Helpfully, Bonnie tried to demonstrate how, but no amount of pulling or pushing revealed the secret. Giving the heap a final hefty kick, she puffed.

"Gee folks, guess I dunno."

By then the landlord's indisposition no longer completely incapacitated him — he had sobered up a little. Dark haired, gaunt, of medium height, he spoke English with a foreign/ Welsh accent owing to his having been a prisoner-of-war in Wales. He ignored my pregnancy. Did we want the flat? We didn't really . . . but . . . "Yes." it would be cheaper than staying in a motel, while looking for something else, even if the prospect of living there at first (and second and third) appalled us. The landlord, Franc, poured out his troubles: his wife, originally from London (England, not Ontario), had disappeared, taking their young son and her father away in the family Buick . . . "If only she hadn't taken the car," he sighed.

Not giving him time to change his mind, we humped all our paraphernalia up two flights of stairs, which took ages. Exhausted. Hot. Hungry. Thirsty. By the time we had seen to those needs it was growing dark. We discovered how to convert the bed-settee into a bed, but it was on two levels — honest! — one half was a good six inches higher (or lower!) than the other and a mass of broken springs. Twang, twang was met by snap, snap from Jeff's pliers — it resembled a bed of nails like that used by a fairground fakir.

Next morning Jeff set out early looking for work and within the day he got a job with Vancouver Motors, the biggest Ford dealers in Canada, as a garage assistant at a much better salary than he had been getting in Toronto. He was to start immediately. Things were looking up for him. He deserved it. In the past couple of weeks he had shown himself to be a fantastic driver, and he just loved working with cars.

He escaped each day from our suite; I don't know why he did it with such alacrity; life there was anything but humdrum. Bonnie and Jon were British Columbians though not from Vancouver and another young couple, Anna and Josef, she also pregnant, were Ukranian/Canadians. With three rotund girls waddling in and out of the house it was to be expected (no pun intended) that the neighbours were convinced that it was a refuge for unmarried mothers. Some refuge!

My newfound friends, whose babies were due before ours, concerned about my well-being, advised me about medical care. I registered with St. Paul's Hospital in Burrard Street, down-town Vancouver, and was given there the name of a general practitioner, who would attend the birth; his office was a short bus-ride away from our flat. I contacted him. Learning that I was not covered financially for medical care, he asked how we would be paying and explained, in case I did not know already, that bills had to be met promptly. I got the message! We had sufficient cash left in savings to pay these bills, but not much extra. I did not enquire what the procedure would have been if we had no money. Maybe we would have to sell the baby?

A few days later, there was a General Election and, contrary to all the predictions, the Progressive Conservatives gained sufficient seats to win and John Diefenbaker, their leader, became the Premier, ending long years of Liberal Pary rule in Canada. Diefenbaker, installed in the capital of Canada, Ottawa, hailing as he did from the West, previous prime ministers had been from Quebec or Ontario, shifted the emphasis away from those two financially rich and powerful provinces. It caused quite a stir.

Which was more than our presence was doing; Bonnie and Anna and their spouses were duly agog at what we had undertaken and achieved but, apart from that, our arrival on the Pacific Coast caused not a ripple — just like our departure from Toronto. We were nobodies — didn't exist, except when it came to paying for medical treatment! Maybe we should have contacted The Vancouver Sun to tell our story: a young couple abandoning life in thriving Toronto for less up-to-date Vancouver (the adjectives: Torontonian in origin) but we didn't. Mr Diefenbaker going East, we thought, would be more newsworthy than our trek West!

Jeff's first priority had been to find a job; mine to sort out maternity care. That done, and a semblance of order established in our bed-sitting-room, we had time to cast our minds back over the past weeks to relive the trip and rejoice in its successful completion. Our new friends were amazed by our adventure; east of the Rockies was another world to them. We wrote to Eva and Ben saying Vancouver was all we had hoped for; we loved the place already. Using my diary, I wrote a detailed account of our journey to our families, though many of the happenings were so imprinted on my mind I didn't need a written source to prompt me!

With little impression on the appearance of our rooms, I attempted to clean up the suite. There was no running water in the flat, and no hot water available anywhere, therefore, it was a case of drawing water in the bathroom to heat on the stove. With no labour saving devices of any kind, not even a fridge, my days were taken up with chores; shopping daily for perishable foodstuffs; looking for baby clothes; or, making them on my hand-operated sewing machine; exchanging chat with Bonnie and Anna; above all scouring advertisements and making telephone calls, with futile results, in an endeavour to find alternative accommodation. We spent long hours discussing our babies and the equipment we had yet to buy. Their preparations were not much further advanced than mine, which I found encouraging, because they didn't have the excuse of being new arrivals. Unlike us, they wouldn't have any medical expenses to pay but, surprisingly, they didn't appear to have any more spare cash than we had; neither of their husbands had a full-time, permanent job and, in common with a lot of people, they found it difficult to maintain a comfortable lifestyle. But they *did* have one advantage, which, with the weeks slipping by, I began to *crave:* parents and relatives on hand. Missing Eva's support, I felt very vulnerable.

We lived close to one of Vancouver's seven bathing beaches (all of them within fifteen minutes of the city) and in the evenings Jeff and I would go for a stroll along the sand or sit on one of the many long tree trunks used for seating on the beach, to revel in the picturesque surroundings; at the same time bemoaning our inability to find a suitable place to live. There was a great shortage of inexpensive accommodation. As time passed we became very worried indeed.

Vancouver was named after Captain George Vancouver, who sailed into what is now Burrard Inlet in 1792. The entire area was densely wooded and remained like that for a hundred years. The railways had opened up Canada, creating a nation as the tracks ran westwards. "The railway made this country," a fellow had said to us when we lingered for a chat, while getting gas at a service station next to the Trans-continental rail-line. The prairie towns and villages owed their very existence to the coming of the trains. West of Swift Current, Saskatchewan, no town predates the railway. British Columbia, cut off from the rest of the continent by the Rockies, was originally going to join the USA but the coming of the railroad made them join Canada. In the early years, New Westminster, near Vancouver, was the province's capital; later Victoria, on Vancouver Island, became the seat of the provincial parliament. The first train did not reach Vancouver until 1886, which was still at that time just a clearing in a forest. A shack-town developed and seventy years later we had this lovely city, where we would make our home – we hoped! The third largest city in Canada, after Montreal and Toronto, it was a young city. The first *white* woman to be born in the place was still living there! In time the construction of the Trans-continental Highway would reduce the importance of the Trans-Canada passenger trains, though the railways are still vital for the movement of freight. Vancouver was the western terminus of the famous oil pipeline, which tapped the fabulous oil fields of Alberta. With berths for forty-five ocean-going vessels, passenger and cargo ships from all over the world bustled in and out of the port.

There was wealth, but also the opposite, even for non-emigrants. In our search for an apartment we viewed many as poorly furnished as ours, though maybe they didn't have the ongoing entertainment!

Franc claimed that worry prevented him from going to work. The telephone rang incessantly. He refused to answer it. Debt collectors for mortgage, car, TV . . . grew ever more impatient and belligerent. We couldn't leave the phone off the hook because, like many of the telephones in Vancouver, it was a party line. Eventually the calls dwindled; the prospective collectors came in person. The comments of the nastier ones, when on successive visits they were intercepted each time by a different pregnant woman, are better not repeated.

The payments on the Buick were long overdue. "Why should I pay instalments on a car I haven't got?" argued Franc, logically, considering his inebriated state.

Unable to get a decent night's sleep after a busy day, I became very tired. The higher section of the bed had the lesser number of broken springs, but it was on a slight tilt towards the floor; whenever I relaxed fully I rolled off.

But relief was on the way. Eva and Ben had decided life without us wasn't worth living, or something like that, and were en route to join us in Vancouver, until, that was, they contacted us to say they weren't. The big end had gone in their car, two hundred miles out from Toronto. They were going to limp back there, but already their furniture was on its way by rail to Vancouver. Could we do something about it?

Franc was now sleeping on a mattress on the basement floor, because he had let *his* flat to a newly-landed family from England. He gladly gave us permission to have Ben's furniture in our suite. Now he could have our springless, split-level bed.

With effusive gratitude he said we could use his washing-machine which was also in the basement. It looked quite harmless; it was not until it was put into contact with electricity that it displayed its unique powers, quite magical they were. Once the current was switched on and the agitator released the machine did a quickstep around the basement: slow-slow, quick-quick, slow-slow, until we learned to tie the machine to one of the ceiling uprights, praying that the vibration wouldn't dislodge the beam to bring the whole house toppling down. It was capable of doing a family wash on a *dessertspoonful* of detergent. We made that discovery on our first use of the machine, when someone tossed in a couple of cups of washing powder and switched it on. Two of us retreated to the chores upstairs. A few minutes later, a piercing scream from Anna, who was laundress-in-charge, brought us belting downstairs again. A tidal wave of frothing foam was advancing across the floor, while the machine, belching forth steam and oozing bubbles from under its lid, seemed to be a victim of St. Vitus's dance as it jerked its awkward bulk around the basement in time to the noisy clic-clack, clic-clack, of the agitator.

"Don't just stand there laughing," shrieked Anna above the frightful din. Tall, blonde Anna was not her usual dignified self. "Do something!" she yelled.

I switched off the machine. That stopped its gyrations.

"Say, watcha reckon went wrong?" asked a puce-faced Anna, knee deep in suds.

"Guess we put in too much powder," Bonnie giggled.

"Pretty fierce agitator, economical machine though," I said.

"Oh shut up you two," bellowed Anna irritably. "It's nothin' to joke about. If it does that with the soap, whacha think it's done to the clothes?"

They were all right *and* the basement floor had never been cleaner.

Seven months previously, not owning a vehicle, we had got to know Toronto by riding the street-cars between places of interest. Here, we were more fortunate in having our own transport. At weekends, in between scouting for alternative quarters, we would go for short drives. Within easy reach of the city it was possible to go snow skiing and outdoor swimming on the same day; needless to say, we didn't do either, but there was much of interest to experience with little financial outlay, which was great. A favourite haunt was Stanley Park, a park without gates — 'a place of beauty for everyone to enjoy'. It was and we did. The forest of spruce, cedar, pine, hemlock, Douglas fir — some of which were *nine hundred* years' old — had five miles of bridle trails through them, which were not used by us, but we did ramble along short stretches of the twenty-two miles of footpaths, or drove around the eleven miles of road. Direction signs were cut into heavy logs in keeping with the surroundings. With boating facilities at the Lost Lagoon; famous Totem poles to study; rose gardens; even cricket!; a good-sized zoo contained, from the Falkland Islands, the only king penguins in Canada, polar and grizzly bears, monkey island, an aviary and much more; Brocton Point Lighthouse, where the nine o'clock gun, fired by electricity, boomed each evening: it could be heard seven miles away; Prospect Point overlooking the busy shipping lanes; restaurants — or picnic areas for the less-well-off, like us! — an open air theatre, there was plenty of entertainment, which we varied from week to week.

Sometimes we drove over the bridge and through West Vancouver to Horseshoe Bay, where ferries to and from Vancouver Island, other islands, or Coastal British Columbia departed and arrived. Nearby was Whytecliff, whose wooded cliffs descended to the waters of Howe Sound, a magnificent viewpoint, sixteen miles from the city. Amazing as it might seem now, there were no roads in British Columbia north of that point. From that location, today, runs a highway with spectacular scenery to the world-famous ski centre at Whistler Mountain seventy miles to the north of Vancouver. Other times we remained south of English Bay, our side, and took a ride along Marine Drive to the University of British Columbia to stroll around the campus while admiring the prospect across the bay to Howe Sound and the Gulf of Georgia with its encircling Coast Range Mountains, stopping to look at the huge totem poles carved by Indians of the Squamish Tribe, before returning, often by way of Queen Elizabeth Park atop Little Mountain with views over the city, to the anything-but-beautiful flat.

Conditions on the home front worsened. Quite unexpectedly, Mrs Franc returned. She was a hefty woman with a voice to match. We sensed trouble. We weren't wrong. Within half-an-hour of the family reunion, chaos reigned. The English couple and their two children, to whom Franc had let his flat, were evicted, there and then, in the late evening — their belongings dumped outside, and they had nowhere to go. We found out afterwards that they never recovered their month's rent: they could not afford to take legal proceedings.

We were berated at length for bringing Ben's furniture into the flat and putting her divan — so that's what it was! — to rot in the basement. She insisted we had to have it back in our room. "Yes, right now, tonight." Thank goodness she couldn't force us to sleep on it!

"Why don't you go to bed, father?" she snapped irritably at the timid man hovering in the background.

"I can't," he protested. "There's a *man* in my bed." In the confusion we had all forgotten Ed, another new tenant, who had retired early. Grandpa, unselfishly, offered to share his bed with him, but Ed didn't fancy the idea, just dressed hurriedly and departed into the night.

Mrs Franc, in an aggressive manner, warned us all that we would have to leave before our babies were born. In the meantime our rent was their only income. Alternative accommodation was elusive. Our anxiety was worsening. All our babies were due within six weeks — mine being expected last. Josef had been without a proper job for some time; he and Anna were making arrangements to move to Calgary, where they had relatives among the sizable Ukranian population. Bonnie and Jon had family living in Vancouver, who would come to their rescue if required. We felt very much two against the whole Western World!

One day the snatch-back men arrived with a tow-truck, grabbed the Buick by the scruff of the neck, hitched it to the truck and departed in a cloud of dust, all without being seen by Mrs Franc, but we saw it happen and, later, witnessed her discovery of the loss. Hastily we dived for cover to escape her wrath.

Grandpa was general factotum. The furnace, which supplied the hot water, was an ancient sawdust-burning contraption, but there was no sawdust nor money to buy any. He kept smoke signals spiralling by burning stacks of old newspapers and any wood he could lay his hands on, even driftwood from the beaches and, on one occasion, someone's timber for a bookcase. It wasn't only the boiler which generated heat then. With hot water available, he was also washerman. Not for him any sorting, or suiting the water temperature to the fabric. Everything was dumped in together, pushed under water with a stout stick and boiled rapidly. Consequently his lines of washing displayed no rainbow hues, but all articles were various shades of the same colour. Blue one week. Green the next. It gave us all a good laugh.

I was much less amused one day when, instead of my white washing, I produced a machine-load of pink. The culprit? One of Grandpa's red socks trapped under the agitator.

We had lived there for over five weeks, when, one Sunday, it all got too much for me. The noisy arguments between husband and wife, sometimes with actions, had gone on for days. I had had as much as I could take. I broke down. I cried and cried. Poor Jeff fussed around me, but I was inconsolable.

When my storm of tears abated, he suggested we should go for a drive. Boy! was that a bad move on his part. When the time came to return, I refused to go back. I was adamant. Never. Never would I set foot in that house again. Coaxing and pleading were to no avail. I didn't care where I spent the night — in the car if necessary . . . on the beach . . . I wasn't going back. Ever. And I didn't!

It was dark, after hours of fruitless searching, before we managed to rent a couple of attic rooms. The Austrian caretakers, who lived on the ground floor and were about to retire for the night when we arrived, explained that the accommodation could only be temporary because the house was due for demolition. No understatement that. 'Due for demolition' — it looked as if a couple of accidental sneezes would raze the building to the ground.

Jeff returned for our bedding and crockery and the following day moved out the furniture. Not without a noisy scene; but he *did* get some of our advanced rent refunded, which I regarded as a triumph!

## Chapter Sixteen

"Mavis and son both well," Jeff cabled our respective parents at the end of the first week in August; long distance telephone calls were a rarity in those days. Junior, wishing to participate fully in our stimulating life, had arrived ten days ahead of schedule. How thrilled we were! How proud! How full of joy!

He was a beautiful baby, plump and rosy with lots of hair, pretty enough to be a girl. And perfect. All my unvoiced anxieties, which had been growing in number, gathering momentum, as the months had passed, melted away to be replaced by a deep calmness. It seemed a long, long time; it *was* a long, long time since I had known such inner peace.

Jeff threw financial caution to the wind and bought me an enormous bouquet of gorgeous, scented, pink roses: the first flowers I had ever had from him. (There have not been a great many since; he says that he prefers to give more enduring gifts.) Ecstatic at being a father, always an advocate of woman's equal rights and opportunities with the male sex, before that issue had become newsworthy, he would have been just as pleased if our first born had been a daughter. The babies were cared for in a nursery and he had to be content, in company with all the other doting fathers, to view the precious bundles through a glass screen. Dependable, supportive, loving Jeff, he was my only visitor. Anna and Josef had a baby boy within a week of their moving to Calgary; Bonnie's and Jon's son arrived a few days before Brian. Three healthy boys born within a fortnight to boost Canada's population.

Brian was the first grandchild for both families. We were

inundated with cables, letters and cards of congratulations. For me it was, too, a time of bitter sweetness; an aching homesickness sometimes overwhelmed me with a desperate longing for my family to share with them our new life, our adorable baby son. And we did adore him. We were rapturous. No more loneliness for me. I would have company while Jeff was at work. I would be fully occupied. In those early days I don't think I realised how occupied!

Three weeks after escaping from Mrs Franc, not having found any other accommodation, we were still living in our attic. Within days of our departure the other two couples also made a hasty retreat: Anna and Josef to journey east more than eight hundred miles by train across British Columbia and through the Rockies to Calgary in Alberta; Bonnie and Jon to travel just a few hundred yards to another flat close by our previous abode. Our move had taken us further away from there; we were now nearer town, but not within walking distance of it. Occasionally, I took the bus into Vancouver to have a look around, but I tired quickly and much as I loved the place and would like to have explored further, reluctantly, within a short time, I would have to bus back again, but at least it was an enormous improvement on street-car travel! With everything in readiness for the baby and our accommodation being temporary (once the demolition crew arrived, it would be no more.) housework got scant attention. I had little to do to keep me busy. Bonnie, I saw infrequently, as she, too, was very tired. There were many lonely days. If it had not been for Jeff's company in the evenings, I might have lost the use of my voice – often he was the only person I spoke to all day. But we lived close to another golden beach and the weather had continued beautiful all summer; in the absence of human company I could commune with nature. Here, there was an abundance of it, all magnificent. The bay was always busy with boats. Maybe it would be nice to cross the Pacific sometime? How about Australia? New Zealand? Well, we could always take a ferry to Nanaimo or Victoria on Vancouver Island, little more than an hour's sail away. I would sit watching children playing on the sand and listen to the squeals of pleasure coming from the nearby open-air swimming-pool and plan how I would spend future summers. Adjoining Kitsilano Beach, recently repainted, reposed in splendour The First Iron Horse, a fitting reminder that the city owed its very existence to the coming of the railway. Weighing eighty-four tons, it was the first passenger engine to link up East and West in Canada, when it arrived at the coast in 1887, a mere seventy years before. Presented to the city of Vancouver by Canadian Pacific Railway in 1945, it was revered, fittingly, like a historical monument. As well as admiring adults, it always had scores of children romping around it.

Returning early one evening from our customary walk along the shore, on passing our old Dodge parked in the road outside the house, Jeff remarked about its grubbiness and said it could do with being cleaned. Despite several previous onslaughts with bucket of water and mop its paintwork still bore traces of mud from various locations throughout Canada. Back upstairs, where he gathered together cleaning equipment, I told him that I didn't feel at all well and wondered if . . . but he was dismissive . . . "The baby isn't due yet." . . . anyway he had decided that *now* was the time to wash the car and he disappeared until dusk.

By midnight we couldn't ignore the signals any longer. Jeff took me into the hospital. (And in the dark nobody could see that the car was clean and shiny.) In those days it was not usual for husbands to stick around. Did he pace the floor back home? Did he heck! He returned to bed to sleep soundly and our baby was two hours old before he telephoned for news! But he did come in to see us at the double, duly delighted, beaming from ear to ear and more excited than I had ever seen him, on his way to work, and later in the morning my exquisite roses arrived, a truly huge display.

The pervading atmosphere at St. Paul's Hospital, where many of the medical staff were religious sisters, was calm and cheerful, though I was disappointed not to have the natural birth I had — maybe naively — hoped for: I had to have an anaesthetic (which added to the bill!) and a forceps delivery.

In a four-bedded ward divided by wooden partitions and

curtains, luckily I was beside a window, so it didn't feel claustrophobic. We four were all first-time mothers. Our happiness and pride were palpable; the ward throbbed with exuberance. To be a parent is such a great privilege never to be taken for granted. Each child is a precious gift. The arrival of a first baby, however, changes a woman's life irrevocably. I wonder if that is why a woman on having a child matures, becomes fully adult, can never be a 'little girl' again, whereas there is a part of every man that remains forever a 'little boy' despite the responsibility of being a father? A woman exchanges her childhood playing-with-dolls for caring for a real life baby; a man on being presented with a child, especially if it is a boy, revels in the excuse to play with toy trains.

The babies were kept in the nursery, giving us mothers the opportunity to recover and luxuriate in the peace and comfort of attractive surroundings. In bed (which in those days was most of the time) when the curtains were open we could see only the person directly opposite, but this didn't prevent us from carrying on long, involved conversations with the disembodied voices from the two beds behind the partitions. The owner of the voice in the bed next to mine lived hundreds of miles away in northern British Columbia. She described her life there: the bitter winters, cut off from civilisation; her only means of transport, at any time of the year, from home to Vancouver was by small aircraft; there were no roads. They slept with firearms on the bedside table, protection against marauding bears. Her nearest neighbour lived at a considerable distance. And I felt nervous facing motherhood. I thought I was lonely!

It was usual to remain in hospital for seven to ten days, but five was the maximum our savings would allow. The anaesthetist's fee also had to be paid before discharge. Again, we didn't cry poverty, there probably was no point, just paid up and went home. A few weeks later, when the doctor's bill came it was for the full duration of pregnancy, and not just for the couple of months that he had attended me. On request, he did reduce it slightly, but combined with what we had paid already in Toronto it was considerably more than the set rate for pregnancy care. We were too happy for the injustice to bother us — we had a strong, healthy son. It was only money.

Apart from Bonnie and Jon, young and inexperienced in parenthood like ourselves, I knew less than a dozen people in Vancouver and those only vaguely. Frankly, at first, I was panic-stricken at the thought of coping with eight and a half pounds of bawling baby completely on my own for hours daily, but soon I was too busy to feel scared or lonely. Most times I didn't feel anything except exhausted!

The stairs leading to our two and a half attic rooms were too narrow to allow us to get any of our furniture up them and we had to store it in the basement. The existing furniture must have been installed by crane through the windows. Maybe by way of the rickety fire escape in the days, ages ago, before it became rickety? There was no refrigerator in the suite. Ours was five flights downstairs, not very practical. After Brian's arrival those stairs became the bane of my life. His pram — buggy, I learned to call it — was kept downstairs, therefore, even to put him in the garden for an airing, or a simple jaunt to the shops, meant several trips up and down.

The rooms, though sparsely and shabbily furnished, were an oasis of peace after the noise I had grown accustomed to in the Franc's house. Looking back now, I remember the flat with the sun always shining there. If there were dull days, or wet ones — there must have been some — I don't recollect them. Being high we were not overshadowed by any building so the sun streamed through one or other of the windows or skylights all day and the summer days were long. The back of the house overlooked Kitsilano Beach; the echoing sound of children's laughter; the expanse of blue sky and sea; the mountains across the bay; the glowing light; the warmth, far outweighed the inconvenience of scaling stairs.

Soon after our return from hospital, Brian developed an appalling raised, blotchy rash all over the lower part of his body. There was no way we could afford to pay for a doctor's diagnosis and a remedy. Greatly worried by what terrible illness had befallen our precious baby, I thumbed through my baby bible: Dr Spock. His commonsense advice was given for folk like me, those of us unable to consult a doctor for whatever reason. (How was the disembodied voice from northern British Columbia coping, hundreds of miles from anywhere, I wondered?) Dr Spock was my mentor, probably hers, too. He was a saviour of my sanity on a great many occasions. Anyway, following his printed advice, I left Brian naked in his little cot by the open window in the heat of the daytime sun and within a week the rash had cleared. (Our Austrian caretakers had given us a loan of the cot, but Dr Spock in his no-nonsense-way suggested that a carefully lined drawer would make a suitable crib for an infant.) As I write, I am transported back to that room in the attic. Situated at the front of the house, it was small with a sloping ceiling, the room practically filled by the bed and cot. In the first few days after our return home, whenever Brian slept, I lay in bed gazing contentedly at the tall, rowan tree outside the window, its clusters of bright, red berries luscious against the blue sky. Many years later I recalled that tree, when we lived in a house in England called Penrowan, which had *three* rowan trees in its front garden, but they and their berries were puny and insignificant in comparison with my Vancouver tree.

An Irish name, centuries old, Brian means strong. On hearing our news, Eva and Ben had written to us and Ben had given a character reading for Brian using his birth and name numbers. He said that Brian would astound (that's the word he used and he was not usually given to exaggeration) people by his wisdom and ability from an early age. Cured from his rash, we soon learned that he was not an average baby. Frequently, he slept a mere ten hours in twenty-four, life was for living not for sleeping, but Dr Spock's advice was, if he was contented, there was nothing to worry about! Apart from his prodigious appetite and his ability to make himself heard a couple of blocks away, when he *wasn't* contented, he seemed to be in a terrible hurry to get mobile and see the world. At a couple of weeks he could lift his head off the pillow to look around, checking that I was about: he hated to be left alone; he crawled at four months; walked at nine; and at fourteen months a paediatrician thought he was three years old, but, mercifully, that was all in the future and I remained blissful, while living my happy life under the eaves.

I have never been a noisy person and in the early part of the day, when the beach was empty and silent and Brian was quiet, I didn't play the radio because I savoured the peace.

"Peaceful," snorted Bonnie on one of her visits, "more a sepulchral stillness."

In that stillness, a few times, I thought I heard odd bumps or movements and mentioned this to Bonnie.

"The house is probably haunted," she said, encouragingly . . . "this place sure gives me the creeps."

Occasionally, I did feel apprehensive at being marooned at the top of the big, unoccupied house, never seeing or speaking to anyone, but for the most part, the ten hours when Jeff was away each day flew past, in contrast to the weeks before Brian's arrival, while I flurried from chore to chore, bewitched by my little son.

One day, en route to the basement with garbage, I saw something white dart along a dark passageway. My heart leapt into my throat and nearly choked me . . . a ghost! Bonnie was right! I stood quaking with fear, my blood turned to the proverbial ice, while a cold sweat broke out all over me. I was sure I could hear my knees knocking noisily together. Curiosity, eventually, overcame my alarm and I just had to follow in the direction of the 'thing'. Then I saw it again. Closer this time. My legs turned to jelly once more. It was not a spectre, however, but a white cat! My first reaction was one of surprise that I hadn't yelled out in terror, then I thought: that cat looked well-fed, seemed to know his way about. It swiftly disappeared through a partly open door. Open door? I'd never noticed an open door on that landing before. What about those creaks and noises that I thought I heard at times? Someone must live there? No! It wasn't possible; the house was as 'still and silent as a morgue', Bonnie had said. I was debating whether to investigate the numerous rooms with the tightly closed, mud-brown doors, when Brian banished all ruminations: he was awake and hungry again and loudly announcing his needs to the echoing house.

I forgot my encounter with the white cat until some days later, when I was in the basement preparing Brian's pram for on outing. A slight movement behind me made me turn and there, standing a few yards away in the shadows, stood an elderly gentleman attired in a grey suit. (Yes, in a grey suit.) I really was scared to death that time. Frozen by fright into silent immobility I could feel my hair bristling, hear my heart pounding. The ghost, for I was quite convinced that's what it was, moved towards me. I remained rooted by terror, yet my mind raced wildly . . . what about Brian four floors up? . . . what should I do? Would a scream frighten 'it' away?

"Hi, nice day. Where's your baby?" 'it' asked.

Poor man, I just gaped vacantly at him before stammering, "Up . . . up . . . upstairs, quickly making off in that direction myself.

The caretakers roared with laughter when I told them.

"Guess we kinda forgot to tell you guys about ol' Mr Woods. He lives in a-coupla-rooms on the second floor; a nice man; he's goin' to live with his daughter back East, when this gets pulled down."

And we had lived there for weeks and not known about him or his cat.

I spent hours on the telephone answering advertisements for apartments, without success. Nobody, just nobody wanted Brian. Us without Brian, "Oh yes, yes sure," . . . but with him, "Sorry, but . . ."

One Friday afternoon Bonnie arrived breathless, having deposited her baby with a neighbour, to enable her to cover the distance between our flats all the more quickly. She had heard from someone, who knew someone, who was vacating a suite and this apartment-dweller had a baby, she was 'certain that . . .' but I didn't wait to hear any more, just asked, "What's the address?" and leaving her to see to Brian I *ran* the mile journey. There was no answer to my persistent knocking at this house, where to have a baby was not regarded as a crime. There was nobody at home. I could have collapsed in a heap on the step with frustration and cried. I scribbled a note in big writing pleading for a chance to see the flat and signed it, and to establish my identity clearly I printed my name underneath my scrawled signature, then pushed it through the door.

Later in the evening, Jeff visited the house. This time there was a reply. The occupiers of the upstairs duplex (flat, apartment, suite, rooms — what's in a name?), the baby owners, confirmed they were 'thinking' of leaving, but as yet they hadn't made any firm decisions about when and they expressed amazement that we knew anything about their proposed plans. The house owners were not available.

"Don't get in till real late, you know," they said.

Saturday 9 am found us rattling at the door again. A bewildered brunette in a dressing-gown stood on the threshold, blinking in the bright sunlight.

"Who you wanna?" she drawled, in an Italian accent, stifling a yawn.

We asked about the suite. She looked puzzled. We explained further, which confused the issue even more.

"Folks *liva* in suite . . ."

We asked a few questions.

"Sure they hava bambino . . . babee," she answered, head nodding vigorously up and down.

We gave a brief resumé of our predicament.

"You hava baby, too? You hava? But I no rooma for two babies," shaking a tired, tousled head. "No, no, me sorry, I gotta no other suita," and with a dismissive shrug of her shoulders she made to close the door.

Jeff jammed his foot in it and explained the situation again with a patience born of desperation.

"You wanna *thata* suita," she exclaimed, her voice rising agitatedly. "But family *liva* in *thata* suita," she squeaked.

At that stage a short, burly, gesticulating male, resplendent in a purple robe, advanced along the hallway.

"Whata hel' you guysa wanna at this goddama hour?"

When Jeff had been told that they didn't get home until late, he wasn't told *how* late. Early (in the morning) would have been more appropriate. They ran an all-night restaurant and had just retired for a well-earned sleep! And the reason they didn't have the foggiest idea what we were talking about was because the upstairs tenants had not yet given them notice that they were quitting.

After we had explained further.

"Oh, you wanna coma when they go, but they no go yet.

You coma backa later, yes? When they leava, yes?"

Speaking slowly and using easily-understood words, we started from the beginning again, this time with better results. No she didn't mind taking babies, 'me like babees', and yes, we could have the suite if 'you wanna'. If we wanna! We were so overjoyed we had to restrain ourselves from doing a jig. Jeff offered her a month's advance rent, while her husband, muttering oaths, stomped back to bed.

"But they no leava yet," an exasperated movement of her plump hands.

Now *she* was getting rattled.

"You paya when they leava, OK? Yes?"

"No, no OK, no yes, you take rent *now*, yes?" I stuttered, grabbing the notes from Jeff and thrusting them at the startled woman.

We departed in high spirits. Yippee! Sometime in the not-too-distant future we would have a proper suite in a respectable house. On returning to our attic rooms we realised that, not only had we not seen the duplex for which we had paid cash, but we had not waited for a receipt and we did not know the name of our future landlady, nor did she know ours!

The month's rent took care of what ready cash we had available. (We still had a tiny amount in savings, reserved for real emergencies.) Jeff was paid fortnightly — or, to be more precise as North Americans don't use that expression, every two weeks — and we were nearing the end of the second week. Once again we scraped the bottom of the barrel; it was a familiar and unpleasant sound, but like all our misfortunes, it had its amusing side. I recall one morning when Jeff drew back the bedroom curtains. His exclamation of delight was not for my gorgeous rowan tree, but for the dry weather.

"Lovely . . . good . . . you win," he laughed. "You can get bread."

He went to work by bus when funds permitted, or walked, but he had holes in both shoes — his only pair — inclement weather, therefore, was a hardship. Between us we had fifteen cents: the price of a loaf of bread (we had none) or a bus journey. The need for bread, bus-fares and new shoes was not considered by us to constitute an emergency. Neither before or since, thank God, have we been quite so desperate!

Weeks passed. The caretakers departed to live in a new bungalow, complete with neat garden, outside the city, and the elderly gentleman with his cat joined his daughter back East. We remained isolated in our lofty perch. Due for demolition as the house was, I was nervous in case a hit squad arrived unannounced and, thinking the house empty, blasted us into eternity.

On September 1st, when Brian was nearly four weeks old, our third dwelling place in less than three months, we took up residence in our new apartment.

Life quickly fell into a routine. I had few of the laboursaving devices that many mothers take for granted today, but, mostly I enjoyed my busy round. Jeff was content with his job, which was steady for the foreseeable future, though unemployment continued to rise, and the recession bit deeper. Many people in our circumstances would have lived on credit. It was customary in Canada to enjoy amenities, accumulate possessions, to live life to the full today, to pay for it all at a later stage. But we couldn't bring ourselves to live like that. We bought some items of furniture secondhand to supplement those we had got (and paid for) from Eva and Ben. We unpacked our personal treasures and our rooms became a home. Modest? Yes! Very little in the bank? True! But we had no debts.

The owners of the house, whom we had met on that fateful Saturday morning some weeks before, lived in the ground floor and basement. They were charming, loved children, doted on Brian, gave help if it was asked for, otherwise were uninterfering. We were free to come and go as we wished. They never complained that Brian's buggy took up so much space in the hall; never complained that his voice, sometimes, filled the house. But that might have been because quiet they themselves, were not. Are any Italians? A brief few hours sleep after a tiring late-night session in their restaurant was sufficient to restore their energy; soon the place hummed with activity from wine-making to cooking to building a wine cellar in the basement to 'constructing a sidewalk' — laying a garden path. Every Italian in Vancouver — possibly in the whole of Canada, judging by the noise — if not already busily engaged elsewhere, joined in, if only to offer conflicting advice . . . at the tops of their voices – little wonder they didn't object to Brian's crying! But if there was nobody about to lend a hand, Maria wisely having disappeared for a few hours, Carlo needed music to set the rhythm for his work. He would put a record on the gramophone in the ground floor sitting-room, then clatter down the basement stairs. The music was rather repetitive. He had but two records, both were of Neopolitan ditties. De de dum dum dede dede dumdum, de de dum dum dede dede dumdum he would sing, not very tunefully, while hammering or knocking or banging or sawing. He would break off abruptly, stomp up the stairs to turn up the volume further before clattering down again to resume his singing and hammering or knocking or banging or sawing. For hours! The same two records! Apart from their liveliness when they were in occupation, and they *were* away a lot even at weekends, they were a lovely couple and the house had a happy atmosphere. We enjoyed living there.

We got out and about at weekends, proudly pushing our son in his coachbuilt pram, which we bought from a couple, who had brought it from England, a Rolls Royce of a buggy, compared with the small ones of our friends. Jerico beach was nearby. Just around the corner there was Hastings Mill, one of the few buildings left in Vancouver after the great fire of 1886. It had been converted to a small museum and housed many interesting relics of a bygone age, showing the influence of Britain in the founding of the province.

We did find Vancouver 'very English' as folk in Toronto had said it would be. However, a local Indian Elder had the surname: Murphy, which indicated, we thought, not the influence of England, but, in George Bernard Shaw's words, John Bull's other island!

Brian was baptised at the same time as another baby, who was given *three* Christian names. We had nobody present, but the other family kindly invited us along to their celebration, which was recorded on ciné film. Afterwards we were asked back to view it. We never saw the family again. All these years later if there is someone in Vancouver with three Christian names and two of them are Walter and Glen and he is wondering about the other child and who the lady is who is wearing the funny, flowery hat, it's us!

There was a balcony off the kitchen; from it and also from our windows, we had an all-round view. We could see English Bay, always busy with shipping from trans-Pacific liners to tug boats; sea planes (float planes) touched down regularly. There were glorious sunrises, (we saw many, Brian liked that time of day!) and stunning sunsets; and by night the necklace of lights on the ski lift twinkled against the velvet blackness of Hollyburn Mountain. One evening, about three hours after sunset we had a grandstand view of the Aurora Borealis (Northern Lights). The colours constantly moving, but visible for quite a long time: green, deep pink, violet . . . It was stupendous.

We made new friends. I got to know other mothers at the clinic where I took Brian for check-ups. The staff there were obsessed with weight and I was rebuked each month because, they said, he had gained too much and I was advised to reduce the amount of food I gave him. They didn't have to live with his screaming whenever I tried to act on their advice. Reduce the amount of his food? He had a huge appetite and had been given solid food from the time he was six weeks' old in an effort to fill him up!

I joined a ballet club and got to know folk with similar interests to by own. The members were so proud when their local star, Lynn Springbett, left Vancouver for London to become the Royal Ballet's Lynn Seymour. (Seymour just happens to be the name of a mountain overlooking Vancouver.)

Later in the year, The Royal Ballet (it had been called Sadlers Wells when I had last seen it in London) visited Vancouver as part of a North American tour. Extravagantly, with Jeff's whole-hearted encouragement, I got tickets for three performances. It seemed an age since I had last sat in a theatre, let alone watched a ballet. The strains of Stravinsky's hauntingly lovely music for The Firebird filled the auditorium. The incomparable Margot Fonteyn and the beautiful, classical ballerina Svetlana Beriosova were the principal female dancers that night. It was wonderful to see the company again and the dancing was superb. The atmosphere was spoiled a little for me, however, by a comment whispered rather too loudly behind me, "It's OK, but you miss the singing, don't you?"

Before spring, twelve foot of snow would be dumped on the surrounding mountains, but there would not be a single flake in the city that winter, where it would remain mild. We had frost one night in October but would have none again until March. (Toronto would have four to five months where it would seldom rise above freezing.) The Coast Range mountains to the north and north-east of Vancouver plus the influence of the Strait of Georgia and surrounding waters give Vancouver an all-year moderate climate. In winter it seldom falls below thirty degrees Fahrenheit or rises above the low seventies Fahrenheit in summer with no extremes between day and night. Shrubs and flowers can flourish all year around in sheltered spots. We would see roses blooming in gardens in December.

We were glad we had come. The effort had been worthwhile.

Later, in the winter, when we felt the urge — only slight! — to *see* snow we would take a jaunt with Bonnie and Jon and their baby to Seymour Mountain Park, in North Vancouver, fifteen miles from the centre of the city. At an elevation of three thousand, three hundred feet the parking lot, seven miles from the entrance to the park, gives a wonderful panoramic view over the bay and Vancouver. We didn't go any further than that, after all we only wanted to *see* the snow! With two small babies-in-arms it was much too cold and walking was impractical.

We might not have snow in the city, but there would be rain, though. Buckets of it for months on end. Surrounded by water, marooned upstairs, I would be glad of the presence of people in the house and their music, even Neopolitan songs.

In early November, prompted by local radio, we rushed into the street to join a throng gazing heavenwards at a rotating speck of light: Russia's second Sputnik with the dog, Laika, on board — the world had entered the space age. Now *there* was an idea for our next big trip!

The launch of the first Sputnik, a month earlier, caused

consternation throughout North America, because it showed the ineffectiveness of the DEW line. (The Dew line [Distant Early Warning] was a string of radar stations across Northern Canada, financed and mainly operated by the USA which, it had been thought, would give radar protection against Soviet air attack.) The fact that it was situated *in* Canada caused a great deal of Canadian ill-feeling towards their politically-powerful neighbour. But for the present, with the second Sputnik, the majority of people were more concerned for Laika than the DEW line: the poor dog was destined to remain circling the earth for ever.

A couple of weeks later, I prepared a special meal to celebrate the first anniversary of our arrival in Canada. Brian was sleeping. I slipped out to the balcony; I heard Jeff's step behind me; felt his arm around my shoulder; waited for his observations about 'our' view to match my elated mood. He did speak.

"Is dinner ready, darling? I'm starving!" he said.

## EPILOGUE

For more than thirty years this account languished in a cupboard, although the events recorded were never forgotten. They influenced our philosophy on life for ever. Down the years we promised ourselves, "Some day we'll travel again through Canada."

In the meantime we set up home in England and our offspring increased to four: the exact number we had hoped for, therefore, we didn't complain — well, not often! — during the hurly burly years bringing up a family.

Life turned full circle when Brian, on marrying, took his bride to live in Toronto. We made several visits there, marvelling at how it had changed, but it was not until we both retired that we had the time — and funds! — to consider making a trip to the Pacific Coast. But by then Jeff had had heart surgery, a quadruple by-pass; should we attempt the trek?

By way of a trial run, we set out to tour by caravan in Europe for six weeks to see if, the following year, he could undertake a longer journey in North America. He ended up in hospital in Lucca, Italy and when he recovered a little I had to drive most of the fourteen hundred miles home towing a folding caravan! However, it wasn't connected with his heart, not directly: it wasn't his heart that protested on that occasion, but the aspirin, which he had been taking on doctor's orders since his by-pass eighteen months before, had caused stomach ulcers, that he didn't know he had until he collapsed.

Safely back home, he admitted the trial journey had not been a brilliant success, but maybe we should aim for an expedition west next year despite his setback?

While deliberating on that matter, not wanting my memories to be affected by seeing modern Canada, if we did tour there again, I decided to put my original typescript on disc. To do this I had to learn, aided by Jeff, also a novice, how to use the personal computer/word processor, which we had bought second-hand. (See how the habit of buying second-hand, learned in Vancouver a life-time ago, was still with us?)

Warnings about the wisdom of allowing your spouse to teach you to drive are often sounded, unless, of course, you *want* a divorce. Well, I would add to that: don't let your nearest-and-dearest 'help' with the mastering of a machine such as a word processor, unless you really want the divorce which was avoided previously, while learning to use a motor-car. Make mistakes; endeavour to make sense of incomprehensible instruction manuals; lose sections of text; watch in horror when, on finishing a tiring session, the screen prints the message: Error — Disc Full, and all your work has been in vain . . . do all this *alone* — preferably in a padded cell.

Our marriage survived. My account was stored. The medics gave Jeff the all-clear to travel. We could plan our holiday.

Thirty-six years to the day we set out once more from Toronto in a twenty-four foot motorhome, which guzzled a gallon of petrol every ten miles, to follow the Trans-Canada Highway west. On this journey we had weeks not days at our disposal. Where possible we followed our previous route taking side trips to towns or places of interest, formerly on the road, but now by-passed by it. On occasions a huge National or Provincial Park now surrounds a lake or waterfall or beauty spot that before could be viewed from the highway. We had time to stand and stare and marvel.

Some places have changed out of all recognition; others hardly at all. No gravel road this time. Traffic has increased considerably, yet once clear of towns it was sparse, right across the continent. There were lakes and forests, more lakes and more forests for days on end in Northern Ontario. And snow showers. And in the mornings frost sparkled on leafless birches, at the beginning of June. Open prairies for hundreds of miles through Manitoba, Saskatchewan, Alberta.

Lake Louise, Banff, The Rockies were as breathtaking as we had remembered, but what a different road! We stopped at the visitors' information centre at Rogers Pass, the highest point of the Trans-Canada Highway in the Rockies, for a couple of hours: there was so much to see and learn. The construction of the railway in the last century had been a great feat; likewise the building of this road. In the 1960s, engineers had worked on skis diverting dams, making dugouts: cone shaped mounds to catch sliding snows, constructing snowsheds to cover vulnerable spots on the road, all this in an area of the mountains notorious for its high incidence of avalanches.

We found British Columbia as lushly green (and frequently wet!) as before. And so we reached Hope in a deluge, the encircling mountains obscured by cloud; it had been raining there for a week. We traipsed around in waterproofs noting that the town had changed only slightly; and listened to the roar of the great Fraser River racing by.

The Trans-Canada now takes a less hilly exit out of Hope, so we didn't find the spot where we had had our 'bother' in 1957. Torrents of rain caught in our headlights, danced on the road ahead as the wipers worked overtime. On the car radio we heard that part of Vancouver, where we were heading, a hundred miles away, had been blacked out by a thunderstorm in the early hours of the morning. 'Bother' was encountered fifteen miles further on. It was not our vehicle this time, but mud and rock slides which thwarted our getaway. We had to turn around to join the snarl of traffic groping in the gloom and spray to crawl back to Hope, to leave again on Route 7, one and a quarter hours after first setting out. Neither of us wishes to see Hope ever again!

Vancouver has spread wherever the mountains and sea have permitted, but is still a delightful city. It no longer feels 'English'. It has an enormous Asian population; we thought that, somehow, we had overshot the Pacific and arrived in Hong Kong! We exchanged a lifetime of stories with friends; visited favourite haunts; explored Stanley Park, little changed by the passage of time; took a gondola ride to the top of Grouse Mountain; stood on the open-air stage, now enlarged, at Kitsilano Beach; viewed the city from Queen Elizabeth Park: all the places of such happy memories. There were new wonders, also, to admire: restored Gastown with its old steam clock; the anthropology museum at the university; the sea bus; the sky train; wonderful modern buildings . . .

Then to Vancouver Island by ferry and to the west coast with its temperate rain forest and unspoilt Pacific Rim coastline, its two tiny towns, Tofino and Ucluelet, caught in a time warp. On to Victoria, capital of British Columbia. It was wonderful to see the verdant surroundings again, especially the strangely twisted, red barked arbutus trees.

Because, this time, we were in possession of American visas we returned to Toronto by way of the USA, driving through seven states of forests, prairies, badlands and unspoiled countryside. We visited Seattle, Butte, Miles City, Fargo . . . crossed the mighty rivers Mississippi and Missouri. We lazed on the beaches and swam in all five of the Great Lakes. Ten weeks after setting out we arrived back in Toronto.

The journey of a lifetime? We think so. But that's another story!